The Sourcebook of
Contemporary Houses

The Sourcebook of Contemporary Houses

Àlex Sánchez Vidiella

HARPER
DESIGN
An Imprint of HarperCollinsPublishers

HarperCollins books may be purchased for educational, business, or sales promotional use.
For information, please write: Special Markets Department, HarperCollins*Publishers*,
10 East 53rd Street, New York, NY 10022.

First Edition published in 2011 by
Harper Design
An Imprint of HarperCollins*Publishers*
10 East 53rd Street
New York, NY 10022
Tel.: (212) 207-7000
Fax: (212) 207-7654
harperdesign@harpercollins.com
www.harpercollins.com

Distributed throughout the world by
HarperCollins*Publishers*
10 East 53rd Street
New York, NY 10022
Fax: (212) 207-7654

Packaged by
LOFT Publications
Via Laietana 32, 4°, Of. 92
08003 Barcelona, Spain
Tel.: +34 932 688 088
Fax: +34 932 687 073
loft@loftpublications.com
www.loftpublications.com

Editorial coordination:
Simone K. Schleifer

Assistant editorial coordination:
Aitana Lleonart Triquell

Editor:
Àlex Sánchez Vidiella

Texts:
Àlex Sánchez Vidiella, Virginia Rodríguez Cánepa, Andrea Korniusza

Art director:
Mireia Casanovas Soley

Design and layout coordination:
Claudia Martínez Alonso

Cover layout:
María Eugenia Castell Carballo

Layout:
Yolanda G. Román

Translation:
Cillero & de Motta

ISBN: 978-0-0620-6730-2

Library of Congress Control Number: 2010935074

Printed in Spain

Contents

■ GEOMETRIC FORMS 260

HYBRID FORMS

Introduction: Architecture in a Fragmented Culture

Architecture has always been a reflection of the larger culture to which it belongs. This reflection has been predominantly understood for the past 150 years or so, and is based on the Hegelian notion that all aspects of a given culture are related to one another because they are all responding to a similar zeitgeist. The more clearly a building exhibited key underlying cultural ideas, the more significant it was deemed to be. For instance, Versailles's endless gardens and array of pavilions not only suggest the omnipotence of the monarch, but also represent the idea of infinite repetition, which can also be found in Bach's fugues or Newton's mathematical equations. The logic of Le Corbusier's Villa Savoye, which can only be grasped by moving through it, forces viewers to mentally assemble the fragments of their spatial experience into a unified whole. In this way, contemporaneous ideas about space and time that were germane to the cubist painters and Einstein's theory of relativity are made apparent in Le Corbusier's architecture.

We suggest that such an understanding of architecture is less plausible today, given the rate of change in our culture. With the Internet and social media vehicles such as Facebook, Twitter, and YouTube, access to information has become virtually unlimited. Furthermore, the rate at which it is disseminated is instantaneous. Everything moves quickly and everything changes just as fast. Thus, when looking at architecture, it is much more difficult to articulate any coherent design trend in the traditional sense, because change in our culture has become too fast for any particular set of ideas to gestate and take hold. There no longer exists a coherent set of culturally accepted ideas around which one architectural style can galvanize.

If this mode of understanding architecture is no longer plausible, it opens up the possibility to look at design in a different way. We suggest that by looking at buildings based in the very specific problems they set out to address, the design tools each architect developed in order to solve these problems may be revealed. In other words, with no given "style" in which to work, it is incumbent on the architect to conceive of a language for each project. The architect must do more than just solve the design problem; the design problem itself must first be discovered. Each project begins as a series of questions and forces, and the building that results is the trace of those questions and the organization of those forces.

Thus the possibility arises that the rules of the design can have a direct relationship to its overall content—not unlike the manner in which James Joyce wrote *Ulysses*, where the writing style and structure of each chapter changes to correspond to the subject matter therein. The success or failure of a design depends on how clearly the building is organized, not according to classical rules of proportion, or any tenets of a larger movement, but according to the distinctive rules established by the building itself.

The architecture depicted in this book covers a diverse range of approaches, responding to an equally diverse range of geographic, economic, cultural, and technological influences. Because these buildings are all built within the same ten-year period, and are all gathered into one book, we must be mindful of the human tendency to superimpose succinct categories onto the subject of study, thereby exchanging the full potential of its meaning for easy understanding. We suggest a closer examination of each project in order to discover how the project has set out to define the issues it will engage. The creative and elegant solutions achieved by the architects in this volume are inspiring and serve as evidence that the state of today's architecture is vibrant and grounded.

Unlike the fragmented and manifold nature of culture today, the history of Western art and architecture is typically understood as a clear unfolding of successive –isms: Mannerism, Classicism, Romanticism, Modernism—all reacting dialectically to their predecessor over extended periods of time. This type of categorization was perhaps more useful when the evolution of human culture was occurring at a slower pace, and the dissemination of new ideas was a much more infrequent occurrence. What we think of as the Gothic period lasted from the middle of the twelfth century until the middle of the sixteenth century (in parts of northern Europe). The Baroque describes the art and architecture from roughly 1600 to 1700, characterized by dramatic and dynamic forms, and the concept of infinity. One can argue about the duration of the period of Modernism, and to what extent that movement is still with us, but our point here is that for at least seventy years, there was a coherent cultural conversation that more or less stayed within the bounds set by the manifestos of its early pioneers. With these long expanses of time came the opportunity for ideas to gain a foothold in the cultural imagination and to work their way through all of the disciplines. Thus a zeitgeist could in fact emerge.

What may have taken fifty, one hundred, or three hundred years to filter through our culture and profession is now elucidated, consumed, and dispensed within a matter of years at most. In the past two decades we have seen architecture embrace Post-structuralism, Materialism, Minimalism, Swarm intelligence theory, Landscape urbanism, and parametric scripting. We would argue that these are not even events in a dialectical relationship to one another—they are simply micro-movements that ebb and flow almost contemporaneously and independently of one another, and occur with such rapidity that they can scarcely influence what is actually being built.

In addition to viewing architecture from the broader perspective of the cultural context, it is also revealing to look from within, divorced from any cultural milieu. What we find is the devolution of the guidelines, intrinsic to the discipline, which once governed the making of art and architecture.

In painting, this manifests itself as the gradual loosening of strict criteria governing subject matter. To paraphrase the artist Robert Irwin: "At first, the only subject matter deemed worthy of painting was Christ, the King. Then it was any particular king. Then it could be a man in a red shirt. Then it could be just the red shirt. Then it could be just the color red." In other words, there has been an ever-broadening understanding of what was considered worthy or meaningful as a subject for a work of art. This broadening has tended to have a "leveling" effect on subject matter, rendering a lemon as potentially meaningful a subject as a pope. This is perhaps most succinctly expressed in William Blake's sentiment that one can "see a world in a grain of sand."

Just as artists were once confined to paint only Christ, the King, architecture could only be realized in strict conformance with the classical orders. Doric, Ionic, Corinthian, and subsequently the Tuscan and Composite were described according to specific mathematical proportions, which were also understood to govern the machinations of the planets. Thus architecture was, in a very real sense, a microcosm of the universe, arranged according to the rules God used to arrange the heavenly bodies. Through the Renaissance, the adherence to "divine proportion" was universally understood as the only legitimate way to attain beauty. Buildings could easily be judged according to these universally agreed upon and immutable criteria. With the advent of modernism at the beginning of the past century, all reference to historical language is jettisoned, and most of the leading architects articulated, and for the most part followed, their own manifestos: "form follows function," "ornament is crime," "less is more," "free plan, free façade," etc. Some architects are interested in exploring materials and celebrating tectonic form, while others are more concerned with the exploitation of plastic space. In other words, there has been a leveling of what is legitimate fodder for the making of architecture. Even so, we still see evidence of a commitment to mathematics and proportion in the work of Corbusier, Mies, Gropius, and Wright, and as late as 1947, Colin Rowe was writing about the mathematics of the ideal villa.

Today there exists neither an underlying unified set of cultural ideas, nor an accepted doctrine of design within the discipline of architecture itself. Architects are constantly discovering new elements and relationships to drive the design. The exploration of a building's skin, the relationship between building and landscape, the integration of the latest technology, new concepts in realizing plastic space, are all driving forces behind today's design.

With each project, the architect must now take on the task of discovering what parts of the larger conversation are appropriate to the design, and which of the myriad aspects of architecture are going to be selected as the organizing principals. Design no longer flows from a set of *a priori* rules. Rather with each new job the architect must take on the hard work of *discovering* the rules by which the building will be organized, and then clearly revealing these principals in the final design. Great design is the trace of a question, clearly and elegantly revealed in the medium of a building.

Thus, while we can extrapolate ideas from Versailles that also can be found in the music of Bach, it is the idiosyncratic spatial demands of a challenging hillside site that dictate the form of the Diamond House by XTEN Architecture. To modulate the scale of that form and connect the building to the site, the architects created a pattern abstracted from forms found in natural elements on site. That pattern was then laser-cut into cement board panels, which clad the building.

At one time, the ceiling held the exalted position as the manifestation of heaven on earth. The twentieth century has seen the role of the ceiling devolve into the repository for smoke alarms, return-air grills, and recessed can lighting. But in their Benedict Canyon residence, Griffin Enright Architects have re-invested the ceiling with meaning. Wanting to provide some orientation to the circulation as well as emphasize a connection to the outdoors, they composed two seagrass resin

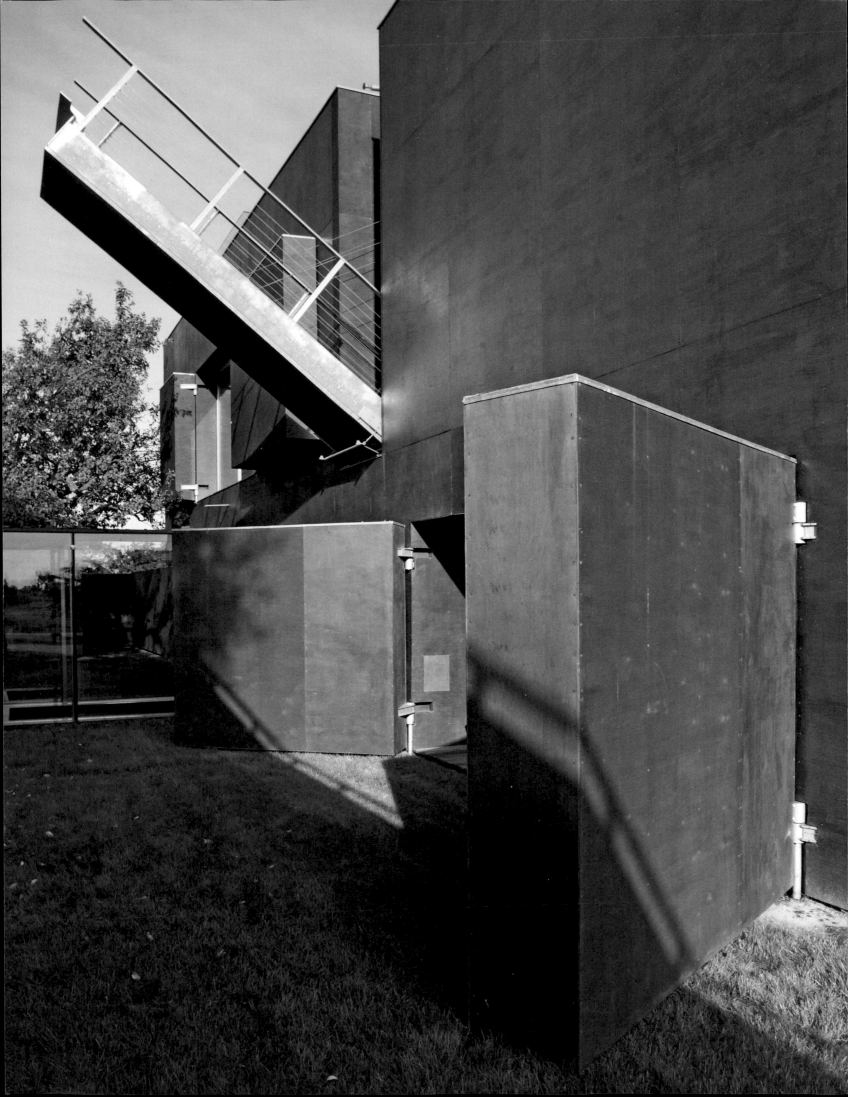

lightboxes, which intersect a skylight. "The skylight reinforces internal circulation, while the lightboxes emphasize motion toward the outside." Thus a very local desire for orienting became the genesis of the design.

Instead of leveraging geotechnical restraints or circulation patterns to generate their design, John Friedman Alice Kimm Architects took the requirements of sustainable design as an opportunity to inform the formal language for the Ehrlich Residence. The orientation of the house and the location of openings were designed to optimize light penetration, and the materials were chosen to be as "green" as possible. Sustainable cement-board siding becomes a tough outer shell, with large punches to reveal an inner shell of plaster and glass. The inner shell moves closer or further from the outer shell, depending on the amount of shading required at any given orientation. An intermediate layer of slatted wood screens further modulates the light striking the glass. Thus the need to control and modulate light, which required differing overhangs and openings, led to the design language of layering, which is further reinforced by the allocation of materials.

Around the world, as the projects in this book demonstrate, architects are looking more to the specific aspects of the given project as the source for their design, rather than working in the idioms of any particular style. Whatever the cause, we celebrate the outcome. The more rigorously architects question all of the aspects of a given design problem, the more completely that design will gather the latent potential in the site and in the program, and bring to bear some aspect of what it means to be human and to dwell in today's world of immediacy.

Eric Rosen is the principal of Eric Rosen Architects, a creative architecture practice in Los Angeles, founded in 1992. He has a bachelor's degree in Art and Architecture from Brown University and a Master of Architecture from the University of Pennsylvania. He can be found online at ericrosen.com, Twitter @ERarchitects and facebook.com/ericrosenarchitects.

David Milner has a masters of architecture degree from the University of Pennsylvania and practices architecture in Los Angeles. He is also a painter and is launching a line of furniture. He has taught architecture at California College of Art in San Francisco, and University of Southern California in Los Angeles. He can be found online at synperia.com and on Twitter @synperia.

ORGANIC FORMS

ISLAND HOUSE

Gapyeong-gun, South Korea   2009

For this striking house, while land-use efficiency was maximized, a sloping concrete structure was laid out on the site following an irregular line on the terrain. The result? The house appears to float over the river. The house makes use of natural architecture in its design. The garden, for example, functions as a space for recreation. The roof incorporates a stepped terrace that mirrors the stepped effect of the garden. The terrace crosses the structure from one side to the other, passing over it and connecting both sides of the garden where the swimming pool is located.

The courtyard contains a water feature and fruit trees, and the garden is surrounded by an unbroken landscape. The interior of the garden is made up of floating bamboo boxes, which comprise the internal spatial sequence. The bedrooms overlook the garden and the home's ceiling dramatically slopes over the hillside.

ARCHITECT
Hyo Man Kim/IROJE KHM Architects

COLLABORATORS
Su Mi Jung, Jung Min Oh, A Rum Kim, Sun Hee Kim (design team); Sung Yeong Oh/MOA (structure designer); Litework (lighting designer); Hee Su Hong (furniture designer); JEHYO (contractor)

TOTAL SURFACE AREA
3,631 sq ft

PHOTOGRAPHY
© MoonJeaonsSik

The architecture of this home, nicknamed the Result, blends seamlessly with its surrounding environment. It is a house characterized as an "island house" and an "architectural island."

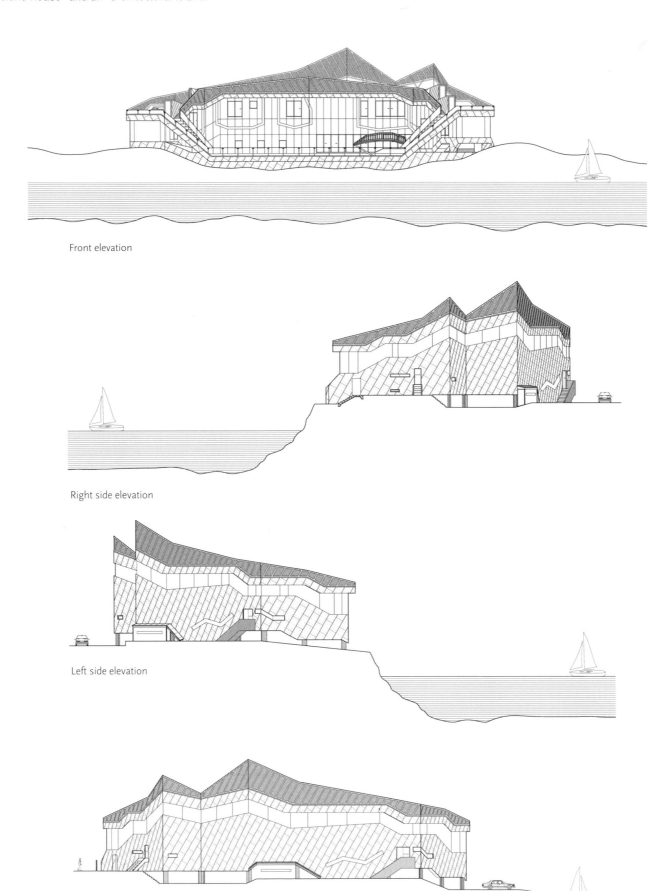

Front elevation

Right side elevation

Left side elevation

Rear elevation

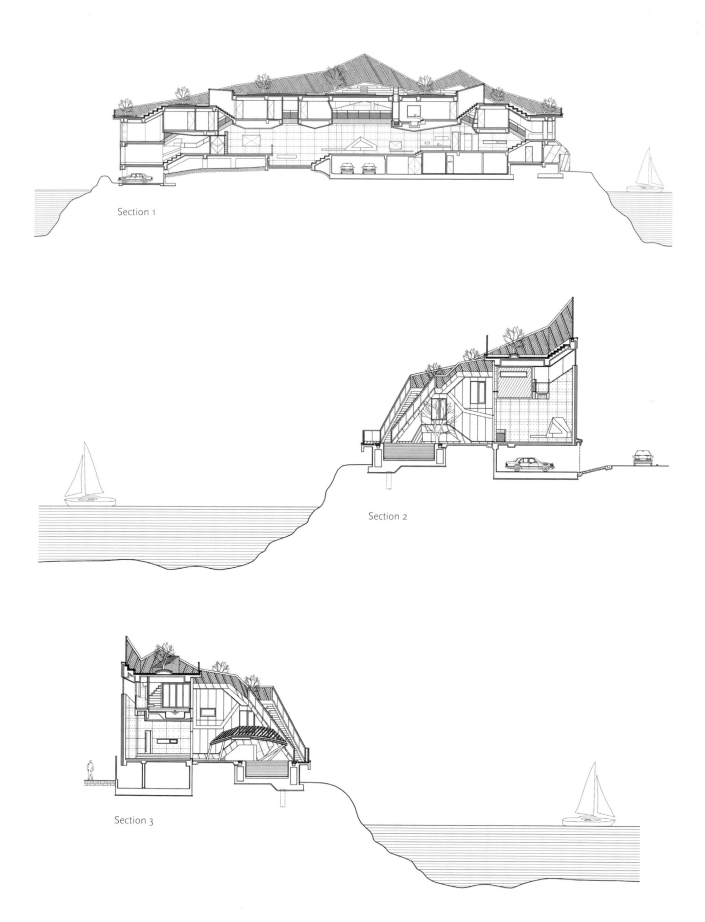

Section 1

Section 2

Section 3

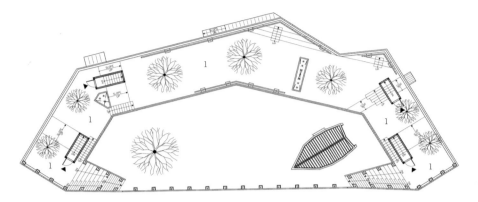

Roof plan

1. Roof garden
2. Fitness room
3. Guest bedroom
4. Pavilion roof
5. Master bedroom
6. Kids' bedroom
7. Studio
8. Studio access
9. Boiler room
10. Swimming pool
11. Main garden
12. Karaoke room
13. Bar
14. Playroom
15. Entry
16. Billiard room
17. Living room
18. Dining room
19. Kitchen
20. Maid's room
21. Service yard
22. River
23. Boat deck
24. Spa
25. Pavilion
26. Garage
27. Mechanical room
28. Manager's living/dining room
29. Manager's bedroom

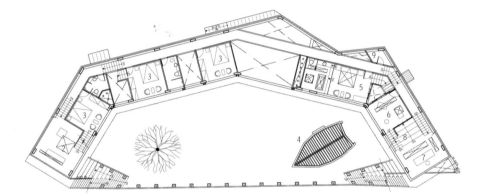

Second floor plan

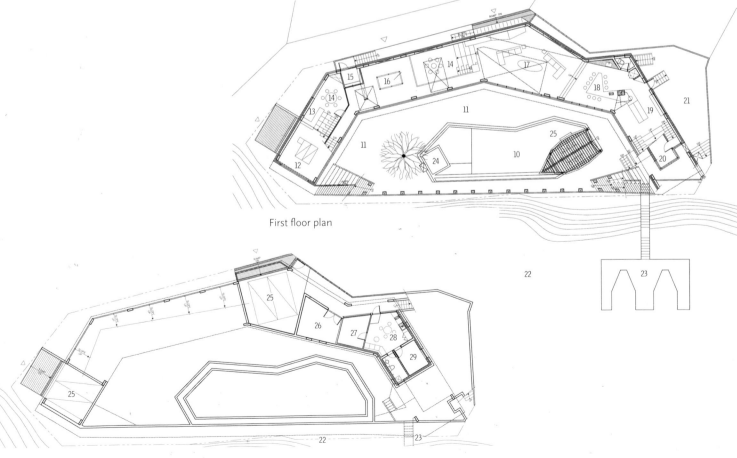

First floor plan

Basement plan

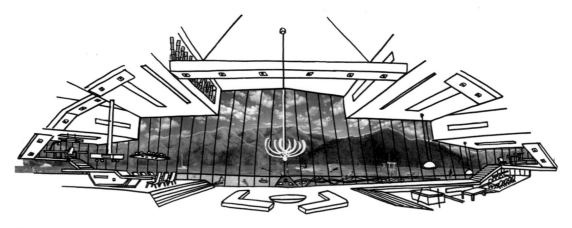

Sketches

Sketches

360 HOUSE

Galapagar, Spain   2009

This home is located in Galapagar, a municipality in the northwest of the Madrid Region. The aim of this project was to create a house to suit the residents' dynamic social life while also providing a place of privacy during moments of respite. The ribbon-like design twists 360° on a sloping terrain, offering privileged mountain views. Design inspiration came from engineering works, from highway junctions and ramps.

Solutions were sought to the problems of plasticity in descending the slope. Even poetic solutions were pursued. The result was the literal building use case diagram, where form does not pursue function; rather it is function in itself. The design was for a cyclic movement, where routine and surprise would become a way of life.

Its complexity enables all points of the house to be reached by two different routes. The curving line of the house creates the greatest possible length, offering a variety of panoramic views. The degree of privacy increases in proportion with the distance from the ends. At the center of the house, there is a completely separate media library.

The façade is black and absorbent slate, a material that is specific to its location, almost aesthetically imposed on the area. The white interior is reflective, neutral, and luminous. Consequently, in fulfillment of the program, the exterior invites visitors and occupants alike to enjoy the vegetation, while the interior invites them to enjoy a social life.

ARCHITECT
Andrés Silanes, Fernando Valderrama, Carlos Bañón/SUBARQUITECTURA

CLIENT
ARCO Design and Projects

TOTAL SURFACE AREA
4,144 sq ft

PHOTOGRAPHY
© David Frutos Ruiz

The design includes two descending paths that allow the exterior view to be admired. Seen from the outside, the house is a broad ramp that twists to offer panoramic views. There is a straight shortcut inside with a staircase offering and impressive view of the landscape.

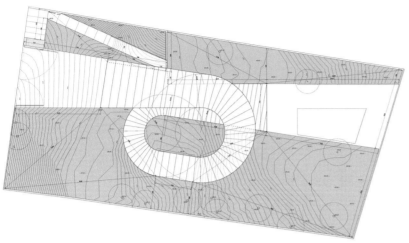

General plan

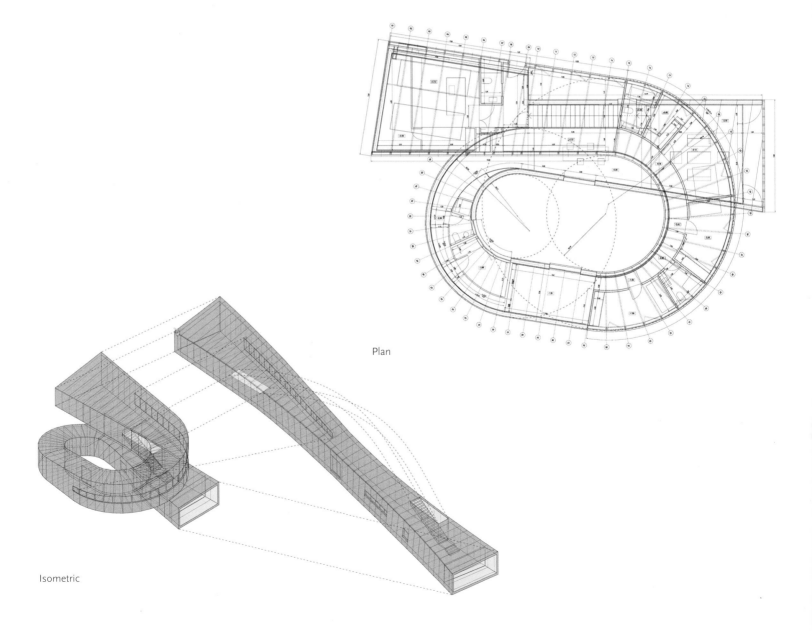

Plan

Isometric

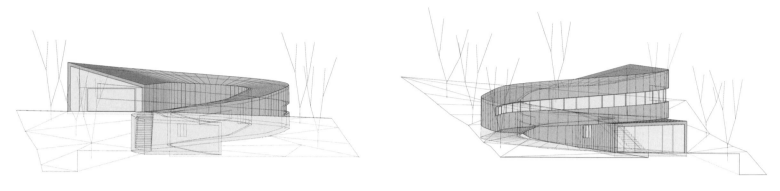

Elevations

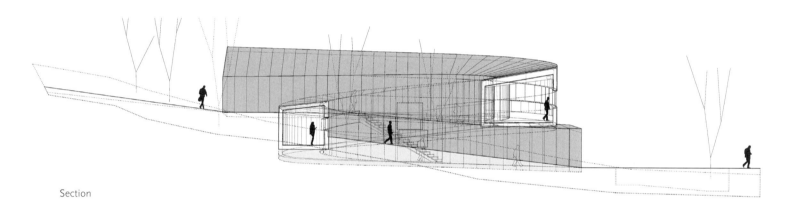

Section

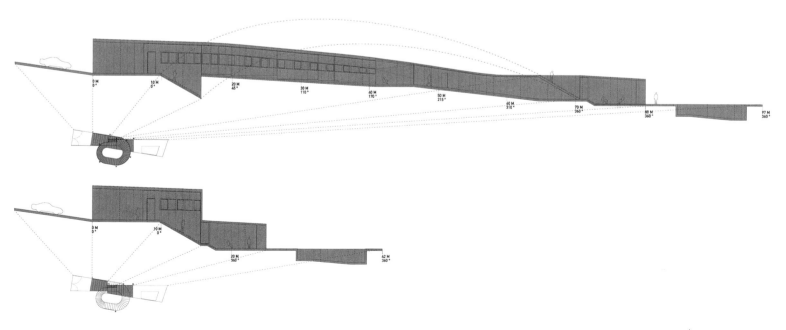

Deployed sections

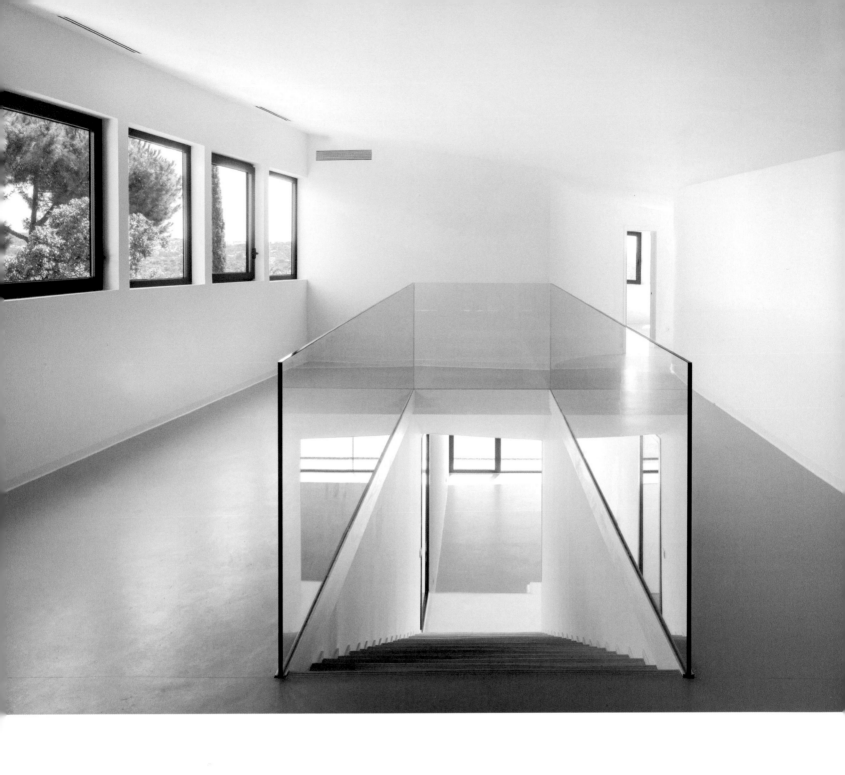

BREEZE HOUSE

Santa Monica, CA, USA   2007

Located in Santa Monica, California, the Breeze House uses an architectural language that takes no notice of the established human comprehension systems. It stands on a 9,850 sq ft (915 m²) site, with which constant exploration was made by means of a program of interior construction and its relationship with the exterior. The result was a building with solidly roofed spaces that open out totally by virtue of sliding glass walls. The mechanical finishing systems were carefully designed to provide a balance between sustainability, endurance, and their capacity for service.

Entering the home can be compared to entering a garden. The entire site can be observed from the entrance, and one can understand perfectly and clearly the relationship maintained between the occupants and the exterior.

The building program placed the house on one level. When one of the 47.5 ft (14.5 m) glass panels is opened, there is an inward-flowing breeze created in an external corridor running around the building. The bedrooms and the office also feature large glass panels, similar in style to the panels used in traditional Japanese houses.

ARCHITECT
Glen Irani Architects

CLIENT
Duane and Rosalie Kumagai

COLLABORATORS
Glen Irani (principal designer); James Caleca, Timothy Grant, Yomar De La Vega, Tracy Bremmer (project team); Parker Resnick Structural Engineers, Energy Development Mechanical Engineering, Irani Projects Inc General Contractors (consultants)

TOTAL SURFACE AREA
3,000 sq ft

PHOTOGRAPHY
© Derek Rath Photography

The home is laid out over one level and in
close proximity to the swimming pool.

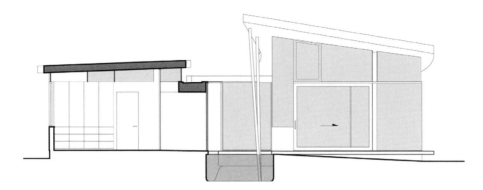

Section through bedroom looking east

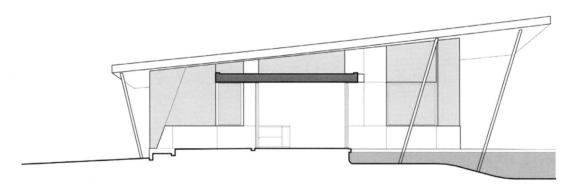

Section through entry looking north

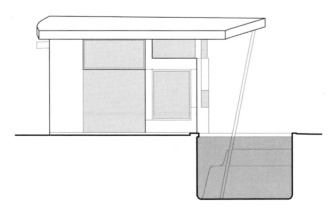

Section through garden looking north

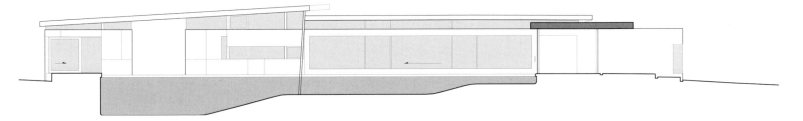

Section through pool looking south

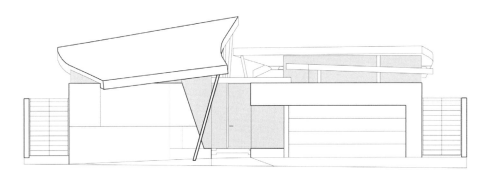

Street façade

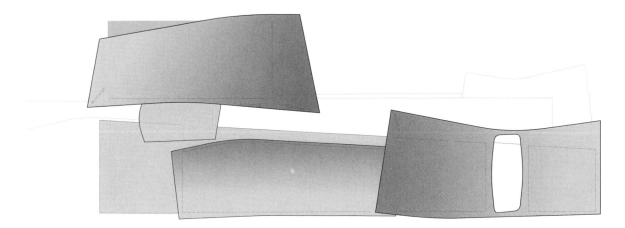

Roof plan

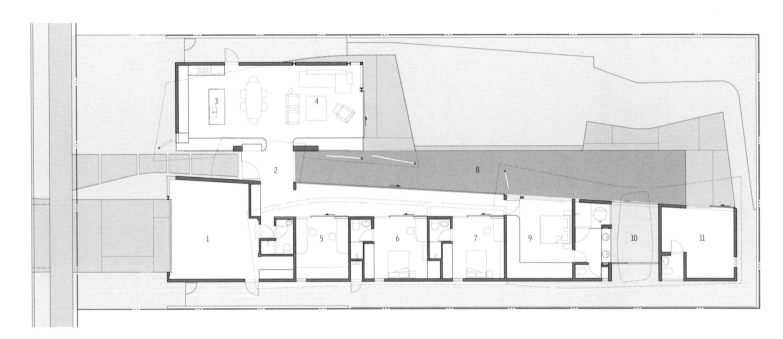

Floor plan

1. Garage
2. Entry
3. Kitchen
4. Living room
5. Office
6. Bedroom
7. Bedroom
8. Pool
9. Master bedroom
10. Courtyard
11. Guest room

DIAMOND HOUSE

Santa Monica, CA, USA   2010

Located on a steeply sloping canyon wall, this project consists of a music studio as an enlargement of an already-existing residence. The terrain offered little by way of access and space for building. There is little more than a few hours of daylight reaching this site. A complex system of planning regulations limited the height, width, depth, and specific configuration of necessary retaining walls. Given these restrictive geographical and technical site conditions, the design and the construction of the project would be very challenging. The enlargement was carefully positioned between the existing structure and the imposing hillside to blend it into the landscape and create outdoor entertainment areas around it, including terraces and even a fire pit.

The construction system was developed to connect this new enlargement with the surrounding landscape and to reduce its visual scale. The patterns on the façade were inspired by elements in the canyon. These were reproduced and molded on the building over laser-cut cement panels. This provided a delicate quality that compensated for the rigid geometry of the design. The lines and forms on the cement panels are enhanced in daylight, resembling the fine ceramic of a vase. In the afternoons, the building appears more voluminous and crystalline, while light from inside the building at night suggests the form of a perforated lamp that illuminates the terraces.

ARCHITECT
XTEN Architecture

CLIENT
Aisha Ayers and Tom Meredith

COLLABORATORS
Mark Motonaga (landscape architecture); Grendel Construction (general contractor)

TOTAL SURFACE AREA
1,500 sq ft

PHOTOGRAPHY
© Art Gray Photography

This building blends rigid geometry with its natural
surrounds through the theatrical effect of its façade.
Made from laser-cut cement panels, it imitates
patterns of elements from the surrounding landscape.

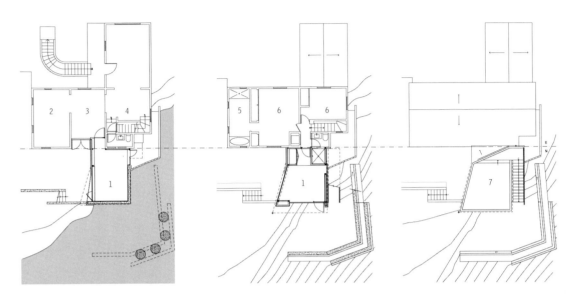

Plans

1. Studio
2. Kitchen
3. Dining room
4. Living room
5. Bathroom
6. Bedroom
7. Deck roof

Section

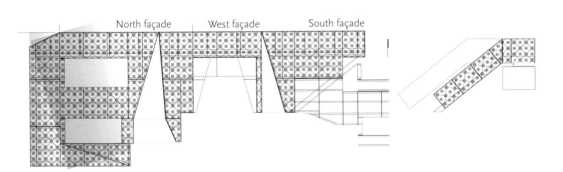

North façade   West façade   South façade

Unfolded façade plan

BILL'S HOUSE

Earlwood, NSW, Australia   2009

This house is inspired by the materials and forms of Mediterranean architecture, more specifically by fishing boats in the Greek Islands. This is the reason why the most important feature of its structure imitates the sails of these vessels. Additionally, it was taken into account that the occupants prioritized open-air relaxation, so the project gives major importance to the connections with the exterior space.

The site posed a challenge for the program. The lot is found in a relatively homogenous suburban area. In response to this, the home was designed as a series of stepped modular blocks, which minimize its impact on the surrounding area. The design was made completely using 3-D modeling software, which enabled the architect to contemplate the influence of the environment and spatial relations. The result was a solution involving a complex geometry of curved structures.

The L-shaped layout lets daylight into the living area, and the west-facing central garden allows light to penetrate half of the house. The kitchen and living area open to a large outdoor entertainment area. This part features a glass swimming pool and a bar with reclining seats. Mirrors and chandeliers provide a touch of luxury, while the backyard contains a vegetable garden.

ARCHITECT
Tony Owen Partners

COLLABORATORS
Joseph Fok (project architect); Tony Owen (design architect); Citywide (builder); Relume (electrical engineer); DAC (air-conditioning)

TOTAL SURFACE AREA
4,844 sq ft

PHOTOGRAPHY
© Brett Boardman

The predominant feature of this project is the rear curving wall, resembling sails. There is a large sculptural internal staircase next to the garden, which connects the different levels of the house and is a permanent source of daylight.

MOEBIUS HOUSE

Dover Heights, NSW, Australia   2009

This striking single-family home explores an ecological and sensitive design style known as "micro-design." Modelling software provides a response to the possibilities offered by a site and planning with space-folding movements. The result maximized changes in level, opportunities for views, and the potential for connectivity with exterior spaces on several planes—a dynamic floor plan. The house has flowing spaces, the direct result of a strong relationship with the surrounding landscape.

The complex geometry led to the development of a new manufacturing and assembly system. The initial design was for a house, but the end result resembled—metaphorically—the process of building a car. It has a complex curved steel design, reminiscent of the human backbone and ribcage, clad in metal panels. It took about twelve months to complete the "chassis," which involved its development as a 3-D computer model, with constant checks being made until it was identical to the original structure.

With a normal house, the floor and walls are built first, with the roof added afterward. However, for this particular and striking project, construction began with the "chassis" of the house. This was raised on the site before metal panels were attached to it to create a frame. The house was then connected and fine-tuned as if it were an automobile, with electronic air-conditioning and other services connected to the central structure through the chassis. Even the kitchen resembles a dashboard.

ARCHITECT
Tony Owen Partners

COLLABORATORS
Tony Owen, Sumir Diwan, Joseph Fok, Lawrence Loh, Mansia Lam (project team); Waterman AHW (structure); Claddah Constructions (constructor); Orion Air Conditioning (mechanical consultant); Site Landscapes, 360 Degrees (landscape architect)

TOTAL SURFACE AREA
3,767 sq ft

PHOTOGRAPHY
© Brett Boardman

This project is a trial for environmentally aware architecture. This is "elastic design," which is flexible and therefore able to respond to the latest contemporary changes related to space, programs, environment, and structure.

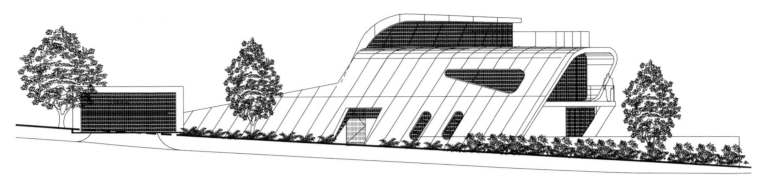

North elevation

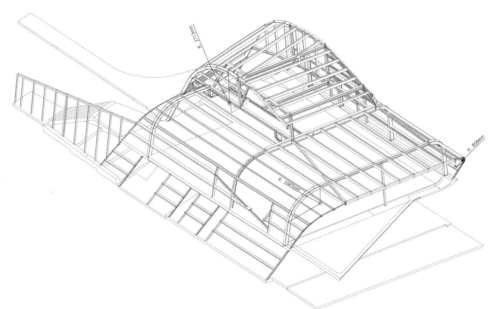

Structure

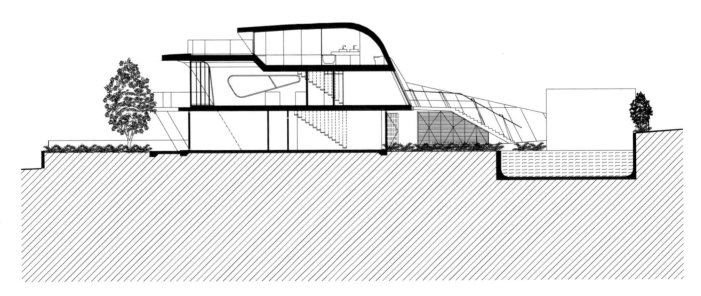

Longitudinal section

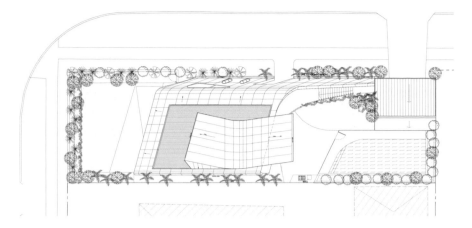

Roof plan

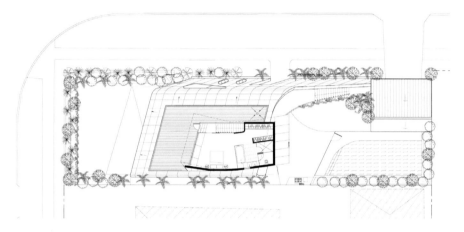

Second floor plan

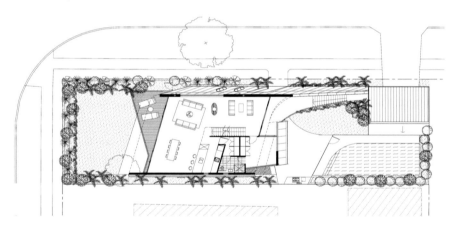

First floor plan

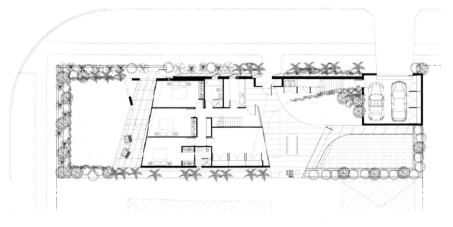

Ground floor plan

HOUSE OF TWELVE

Melbourne, VIC, Australia   2010

This striking home is located in the Melbourne suburb of Kew. The building occupies 5,382 sq ft (500 m²) of the 8,500 sq ft (790 m²) site. This project found inspiration in the ruins of Ancient Rome. More than their historic nature, ruins fascinate by their progressive deterioration over time, revealing their darkest nooks and crannies.

This home is an attempt to imagine a fantasy-filled response to uninterrupted history, following an empirical path through the progressive mutation between contemporary ideas and those of antiquity. Some examples of this way of thinking are present in the horizontal sequence in which the numerous spaces are laid out. These spaces can also be found in classic works by Frank Lloyd Wright. Additionally, there are reminiscences of Gehry's American Center in the front and the public spaces of the residence where circular forms rise from the road. Not only do these openings restore thickness to the façade, but they also enable the winter sun to penetrate. This natural light brightens the rear patio of the house. Unique features of the living area are a water feature and an open vault, lined in golden mosaic tiles.

ARCHITECT
Antonino Cardillo Architect

TOTAL SURFACE AREA
5,382 sq ft

PHOTOGRAPHY
© Antonino Cardillo

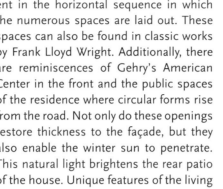

The living room of this home is designed as a "light room"—that is, a room filled with light. Golden mosaic tiles and water reflect the natural light and bask the room in a warm glow.

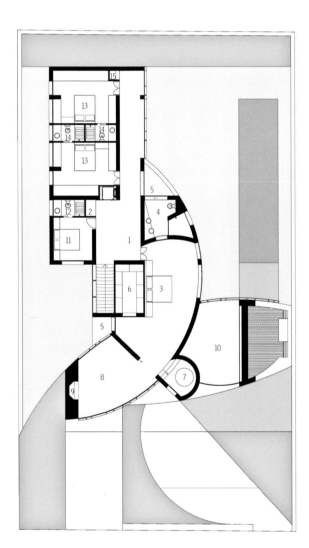

First floor plan

1.	Hall	9.	Chimney
2.	Linen cupboard	10.	Void
3.	Master bedroom	11.	Guest room
4.	Bathroom	12.	Guest bathroom
5.	Balconies	13.	Kids' bedrooms
6.	Walk-in wardrobe	14.	Kids' bathrooms
7.	Boudoir	15.	Laundry shoot
8.	Studio		

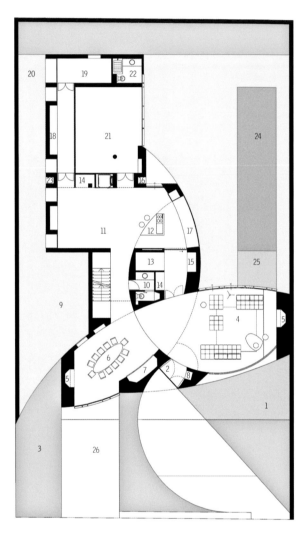

Ground floor plan

1.	Outdoor pond	14.	Cupboards
2.	Entry	15.	Scullery
3.	High hedge	16.	Boiler room
4.	Living room	17.	Bar
5.	Fireplace	18.	Storage
6.	Dining room	19.	Laundry room
7.	Wine cellar	20.	Clothesline
8.	Control deck	21.	Kids' retreat room
9.	Courtyard	22.	Bathroom and shower for pool
10.	Bathroom	23.	Recycle bin
11.	Multipurpose space	24.	Lap pool
12.	Kitchen	25.	Lounge pool
13.	Pantry	26.	Ramp down to garage

CONCRETE MOON HOUSE

Melbourne, Australia   2010

The Concrete Moon House was designed for a rectangular site in a the Melbourne suburb of Kew. It is divided into two formal parts: one space is for public entertaining and the other space is one of privacy. The public area, situated at the front of the building, resembles a rising moon, which gives the building its name. The private areas are housed in a long and narrow volume that gradually form a portico, leading to the garden.

While the two parts seem totally different, they actually have a common origin. The characteristic elements of one of the parts also emerge in the other, although created through different processes. The diverse elements found in each of the parts have a reciprocal relationship. This characteristic resonates particularly in the main large cave, where it is difficult to tell where the shared identity ends and the parts become differentiated.

ARCHITECT
Antonino Cardillo Architect

TOTAL SURFACE AREA
6,243 sq ft

PHOTOGRAPHY
© Antonino Cardillo

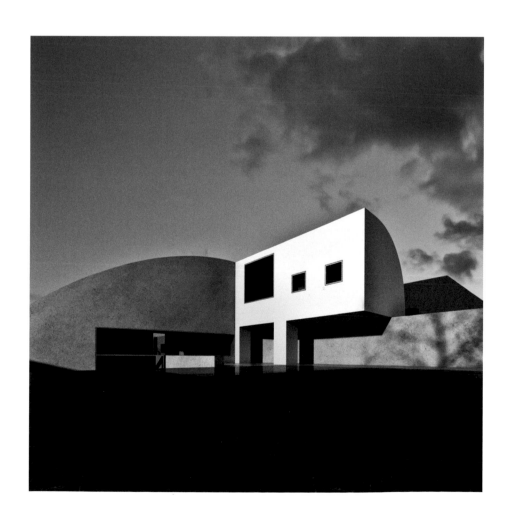

The Concrete Moon House is characterized by the union of two very different but interrelated parts.

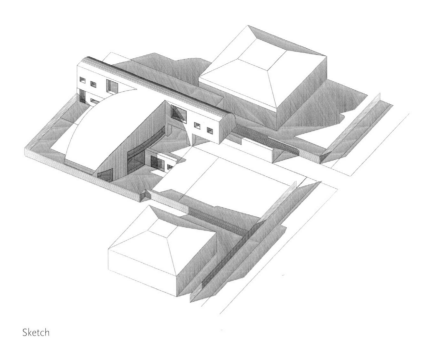

Sketch

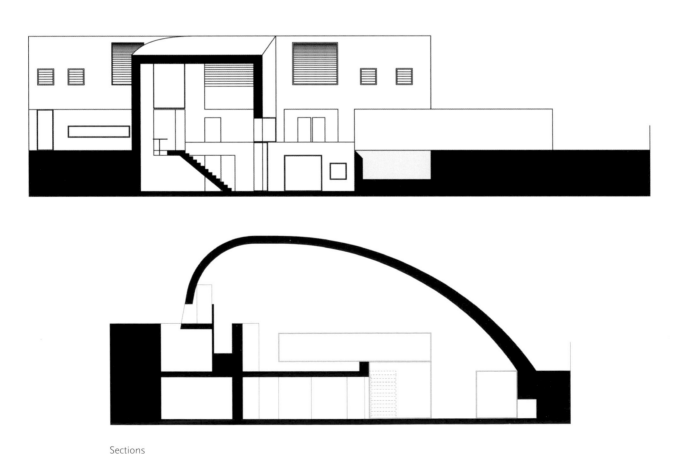

Sections

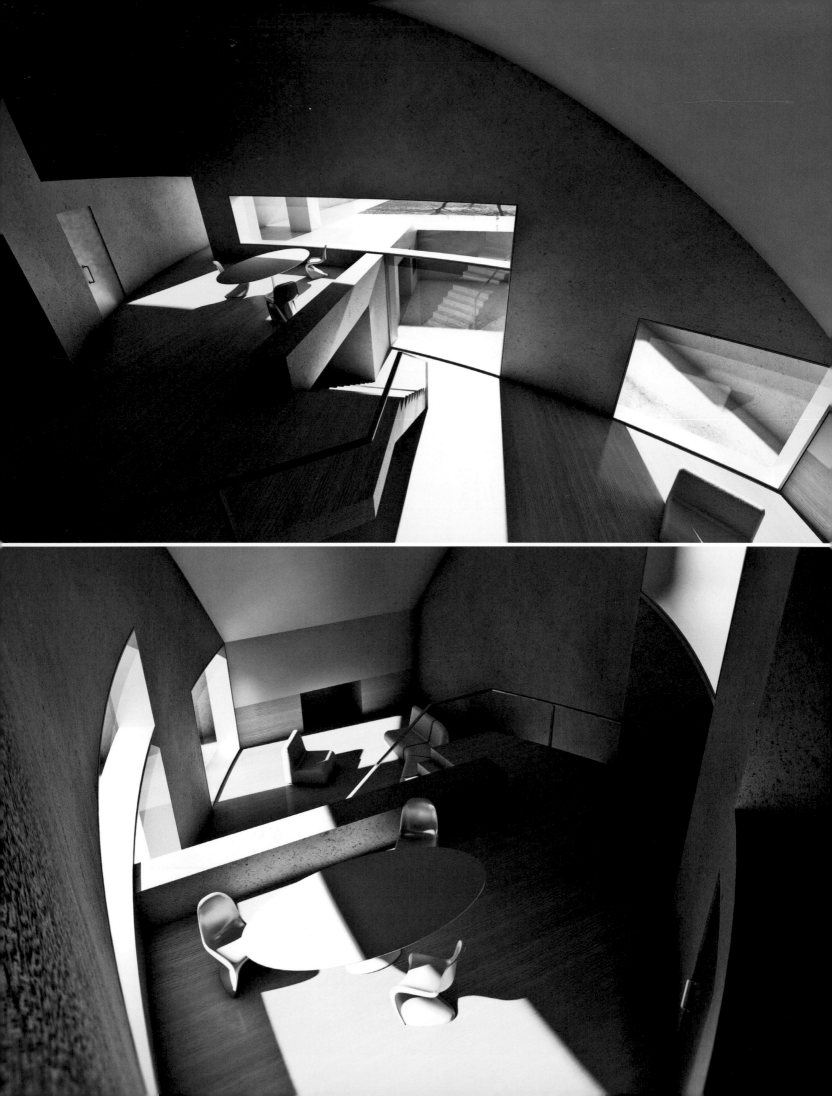

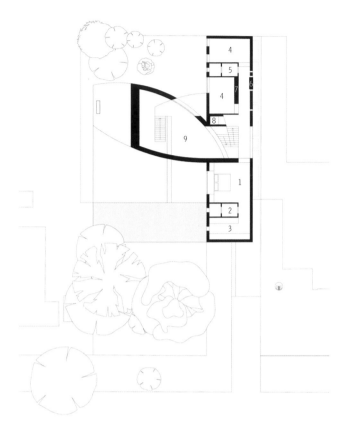

First floor plan

1. Master bedroom
2. En suite bathroom
3. Walk-in wardrobe
4. Bedrooms
5. Bathroom
6. Linen cupboard
7. Laundry shoot
8. Elevator
9. Dining room

Ground floor plan

1. Living room with fireplace
2. Patio
3. Dining room
4. Patio
5. Elevator
6. Cloakroom
7. Kitchen and scullery
8. Storage room
9. Laundry room
10. Bathroom
11. Kids' retreat room
12. Guest bathroom
13. Guest room
14. Bathroom and shower for pool
15. Pool
16. Garden
17. Ramp to garage

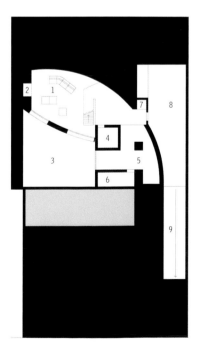

1. Living room
2. Fireplace
3. Patio
4. Bathroom
5. Studio with a private outdoor reading area
6. Wine cellar
7. Elevator
8. Garage
9. Ramp to the street

Basement plan

BENEDICT CANYON RESIDENCE

Beverly Hills, CA, USA   2010

This project called for the restoration of a fifty-year-old house with a surface area of approximately 2,603 sq ft (242 m²) located on a Los Angeles hillside. The inner walls were thrown down and part of the roof was raised, changing the ceiling configuration. The interior finishes were demolished. Part of the original gabled roof was replaced by a flat roof with the same angle, creating a continuous surface sweeping upward. This relatively simple renovation let more daylight into the space and opened it to magnificent panoramic views of the canyon and its wild vegetation.

By blurring the relationship between interior and exterior, the remodeling improved the quality of the space, making it more consistent with its modernist origins. The design involved creating internal public spaces. The new roof was folded and, after replacing the existing stucco wall with a 50 ft (15 m) panel of glass, the rear façade was turned into a glazed expanse that opens the house to the existing patio and swimming pool.

Views of the garden and pool can be enjoyed from the interior. The house is completely transparent from the exterior in daylight, becoming a shining container at night. The garden offers privacy for private spaces, such as bedrooms and bathrooms, although these rooms can be seen from the exterior, producing a voyeuristic effect. The interior space features an open plan, with areas and functions defined by changes in ceiling height, furniture placement, and lighting. A traditional steel and cherrywood wood island demarcates the kitchen.

ARCHITECT
Griffin Enright Architects

COLLABORATORS
John Enright, Margaret Griffin (design principals); Norma Chung (project architect); Yao-Chien Lee, Mathew Gillis, Raymond Shapiro, Taka Mieno (project team); Steve Magnuson Engineering (structural engineers); Revolver Design, Peter Noble (lighting designer); Bonura Construction (contractor)

TOTAL SURFACE AREA
2,603 sq ft

PHOTOGRAPHY
© Benny Chan / Fotoworks

An open shelving unit was designed using steel
columns to replace the original wall separating the
living and dining areas. The piece is therefore turned
into an architectural feature with the dual function
of shelving unit and partition between spaces.

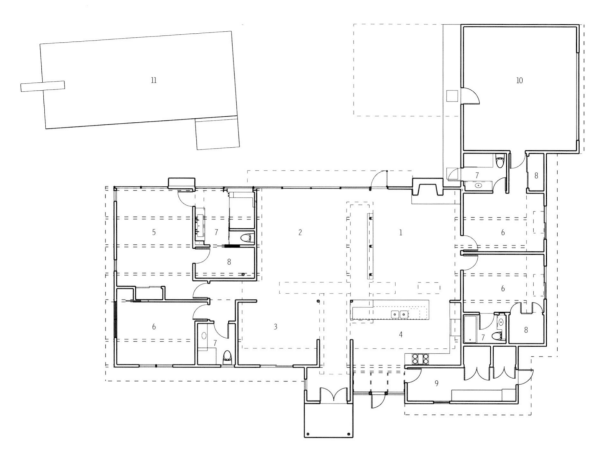

Floor plan

1. Family room
2. Living room
3. Dining room
4. Kitchen
5. Master bedroom
6. Bedroom
7. Bathroom
8. Closet
9. Laundry room
10. Garage
11. Pool

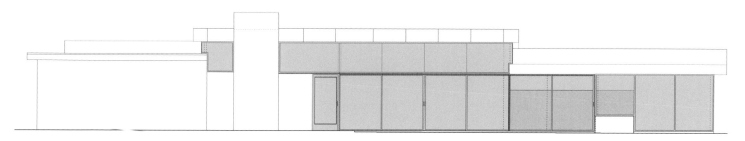

Glass elevation

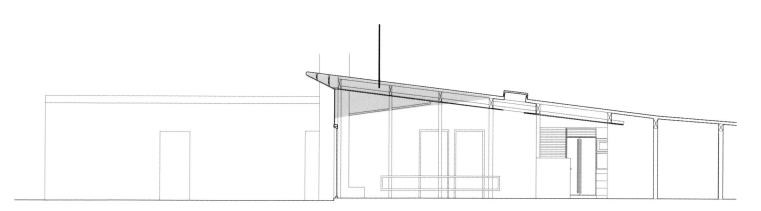

Section and new roof area

RIDGELINE HOUSE

Pasadena, CA, USA   2010

The design of this home preserved the original structure of an iconic Pasadena residence while also providing a new sense of function and quality to the living spaces. Originally built in 1967 with impressive views of the city, this home provides flexibility and a visual connection with the surrounding cityscape. Every effort was made to retain the finest of its original features.

The project was meant to preserve the distinctive form of the planes and folded planes of the roof, with parts strategically raised to allow more light to enter and to provide more space. The west side of the house was enlarged. The walls were shifted and replaced with extremely tall glass doors to capture light.

The main modification was to maximize the visual connection and transit between the interior and the exterior, enabling daylight to filter into the home's central axis. To this end, a number of dark spaces were eliminated and turned into the large living space. Sliding glass panels open to the yard and further the sense of expansion between interior and exterior.

The kitchen and family room open to the swimming pool and terrace, which were also redesigned. The latter features benches and grill islands in acid-washed concrete. The use of plants on the deck softens the design and separates public and private spaces. While the original mid-twentieth-century-style layout made the most of a striking view over the city, the redesign also introduced new connections between the south and west-facing parts.

ARCHITECT
Montalba Architects

COLLABORATORS
John Brubaker Architectural Lighting Consultants (lighting consultant); Elysian Landscapes (landscape designer); The Office of Gordon L. Polon Consulting Engineers (structural engineer); Chris Tosdevin/Bulthaup Corporation (kitchen consultant); Micro Connection (audio/visual consultant); SC Consulting Group (waterproofing consultant); Antieri & Haloosim Consulting Engineers (mechanical engineer); Rohtman Engineering (civil engineer); R.T. Frankian & Associates (consulting geotechnical engineer); Sarlan Builders (general contractor)

TOTAL SURFACE AREA
4,700 sq ft

PHOTOGRAPHY
© Dominique Vorillon

As seen in the plans, the restoration work begun in 2008 on the house, initially built in 1967, preserved the original cross-shaped floor plan. The work of the architects focused on facilitating transit between the in and outdoor areas, and maximizing the visual connections.

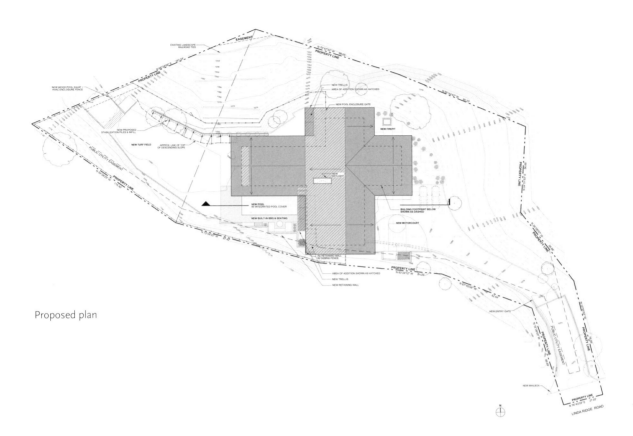

Proposed plan

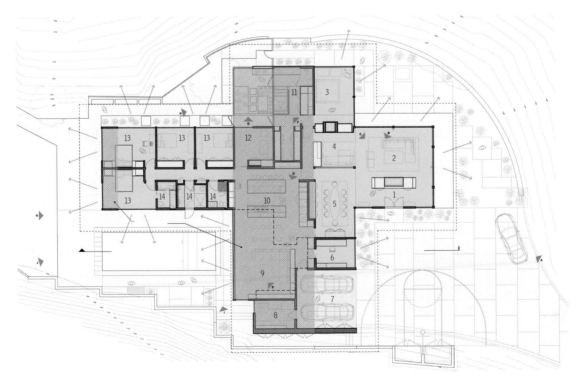

1. Entry
2. Living room
3. Master bedroom
4. Media room
5. Dining room
6. Office
7. Garage
8. Laundry room
9. Family room
10. Kitchen
11. Master bathroom
12. Nursery
13. Bedroom
14. Bathroom

Plan

Existing section through kitchen and dining room

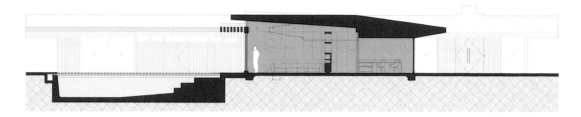

Renovation and addition through office, family room and pool

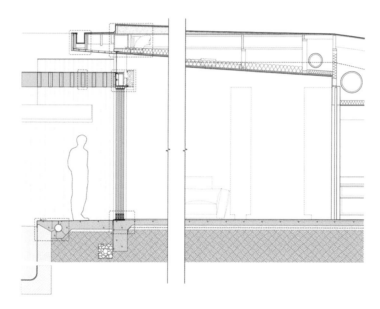

Wall section (family room)

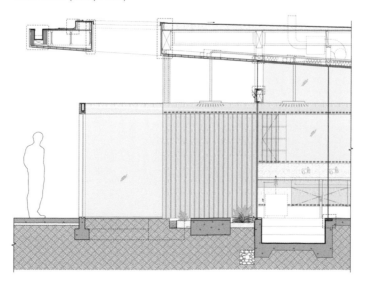

Wall section (master bathroom)

POINT DUME RESIDENCE

Malibu, CA, USA   2009

This house was built on an 6,000 sq ft (557 m²) site on Point Dume, a promontory on the Malibu coast that juts into the Pacific Ocean. The residence makes use of a typical domestic layout, but emphasizes architectural continuity with the landscape by utilizing design techniques that enhance the natural air flow and views. Straight and curved surfaces make maximum use of the terrain and subtly demarcate different spaces within the home.

The geometric morphology of the residence marks its changes through the range of panoramic ocean views. The stepped terrain means the main entrance is located between the upper and lower levels. Here the curved walls sweep the length of the house from the master bedroom upstairs to the living area below. The living area literally opens out to the exterior through large sliding doors.

There are three skylights that form a line in the ceiling and extend over the entrance, the master bedroom, and the bathroom. In the living room, translucent ceiling panels welcome in natural light.

ARCHITECT
Griffin Enright Architects

COLLABORATORS
John Enright, Margaret Griffin (design principals); Mathew Gillis (project architect); Ray Shapiro, Tyler Myer, Andrew Batay-Csorba, Andrew Lindley, Taka Mieno (project team); John Labib (structural engineer); Mark Shamim (MEP); Peter Noble, Revolver Design (lighting designer); Margaret Griffin, Griffin Enright Architects, Marny Randall (landscape architect); Tom Hinerfeld/ Hinerfeld & Ward Inc (contractor); Julio Chavez (cabinetry)

TOTAL SURFACE AREA
6,550 sq ft

PHOTOGRAPHY
© Benny Chan/Fotoworks

The upper level floor plan is oriented toward the ocean, and there is a private terrace off the master bedroom. A walkway extends out over the swimming pool aided by a system of railings.

Geometry of project vs. coastline views diagram

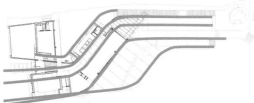

Ground floor plan

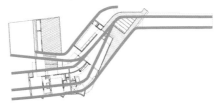

First floor plan

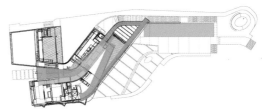

Movement and light plan

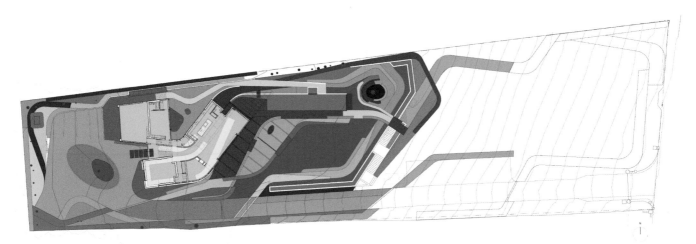

Landscape plan

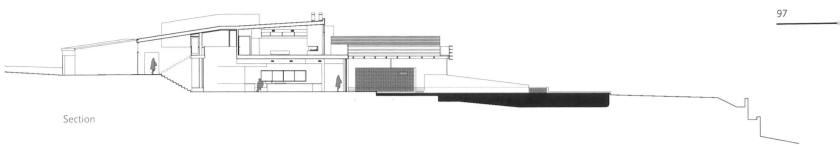

Section

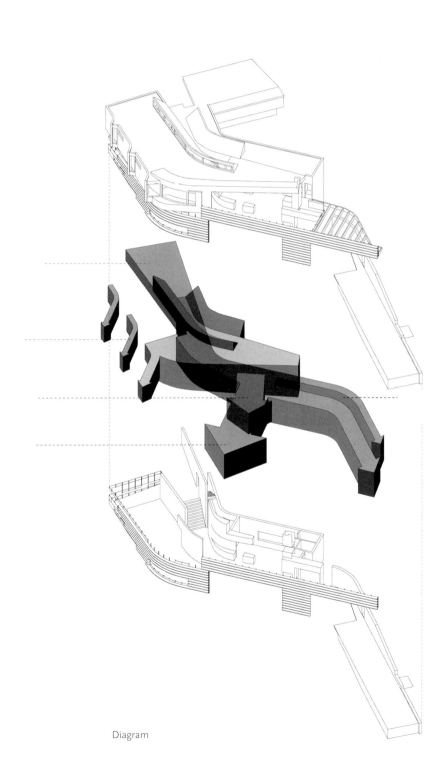

Diagram

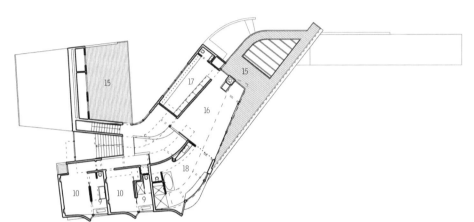

First floor plan

1. Entry
2. Kitchen
3. Living/dining room
4. Library/office
5. Laundry room
6. Media equipment storage
7. Media room
8. Garage
9. Bathroom
10. Guest bedroom
11. Porch
12. Pool
13. Fire pit
14. Patio
15. Terrace
16. Master bedroom
17. Master closet
18. Master bathroom

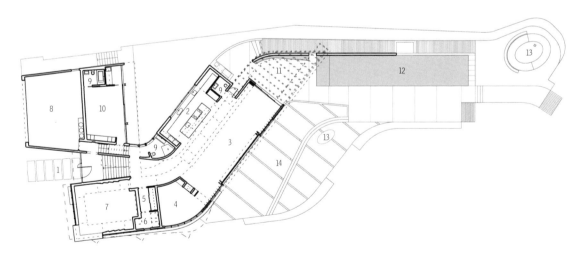

Ground floor plan

MIMETIC FORMS

GRID HOUSE

Serra da Mantiqueira, Brazil   2006

This residence is located on abrupt terrain. A lush forest of monkey puzzle trees form part of the protected area. The house stands in a small valley in the midst of this landscape. The owners wanted a single-story house with lots of privacy and a relationship with nature. Due to the natural humidity of the area, the team built the house raised above the ground.

The design was based on a timber structural grid supported over a series of concrete piles in modules of 18 × 18 × 10 ft (5.5 × 5.5 × 3 m). This grid connects existing transit ways and creates new ones. The structure can be traversed in three different ways. The design program revolves around a core space where wet areas, public spaces, and the owners' bedrooms are located. There are also three separate modules, with two bedrooms each. Voids continue the structural unity between the modules' spaces as well as provide views of the garden. This pattern of voids and closed spaces results in a fragmented layout that offers its occupants protection and privacy.

The leisure pavilion is located on the highest hilltop on the site. This structure provides the home with a place for introspection that also offers panoramic views over the surrounding land.

ARCHITECT
Fernando Forte, Lourenço Gimenes, Rodrigo Marcondes Ferraz/Forte, Gimenes & Marcondes Ferraz Arquitetos

COLLABORATORS
Renata Davi, Renata Buschinelli Goes, Luiz Florence, Adriana Junqueira, Paloma Delgado, Ivo Magaldi, André Malheiros, Luciana Muller, Débora Zeppellini, Marília Caetano, Nilton Rossi (team); Sidney Linhares, Fernando Chacel/CAP (landscape design); Guinter Parshalk/Studi IX (lighting design)

TOTAL SURFACE AREA
21,528 sq ft

PHOTOGRAPHY
© Forte, Gimenes & Marcondes Ferraz Arquitetos

The residence is divided into two blocks that house
the bedrooms and public spaces, respectively.

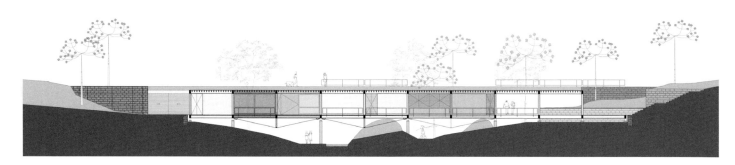

Longitudinal section

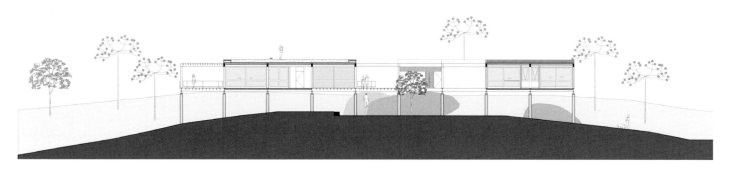

Cross section

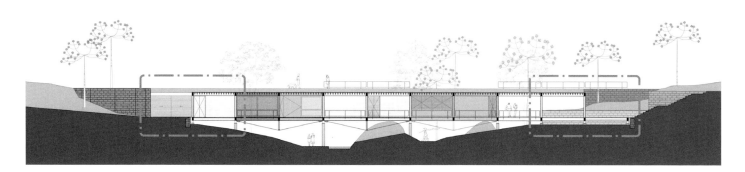

Longitudinal section

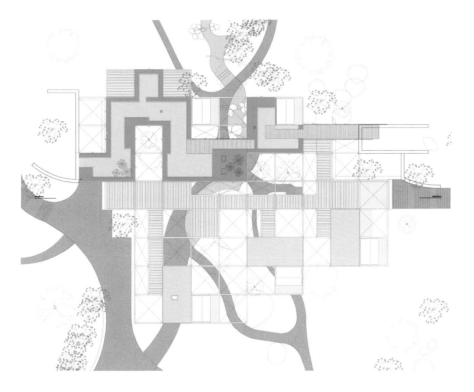

Roof plan

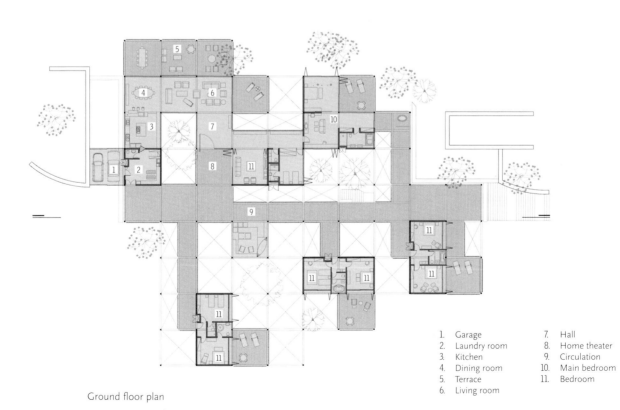

Ground floor plan

1. Garage
2. Laundry room
3. Kitchen
4. Dining room
5. Terrace
6. Living room
7. Hall
8. Home theater
9. Circulation
10. Main bedroom
11. Bedroom

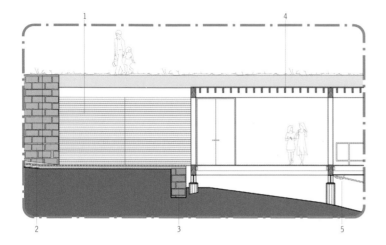

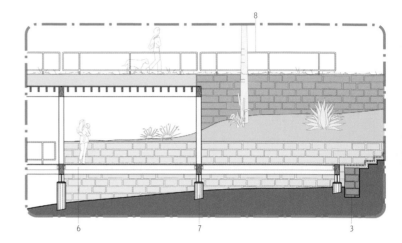

Partial sections

1. Wood shutter door
2. Prop wall with stone from site
3. Stone wall
4. Piquirá pergola 2.35 × 7.9 in (6 × 20 cm) with wired glass
5. Cor-ten beams
6. Ipe deck
7. Concrete pilar 11.8 in (30 cm)
8. Metallic parapet

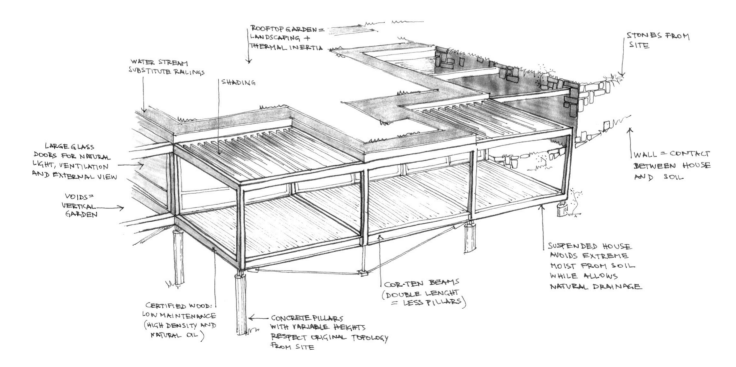

Sketch

GOLD COUNTRY RESIDENCE

Murphys, CA, USA   2009

This residence is located in a valley on the outskirts of Murphys, a town in central California. Designed as a vacation house for a couple from San Francisco with two small children, the house is clearly divided into two structures, each with a surface area of 861 sq ft (80 m²). These structures provide separate living or public areas and sleeping or private areas.

As this house is located a considerable distance away from the local power grid, it was necessary to devise a sustainability program. Structural slabs retain radiant heat, and the insulation panels, used in the walls and ceilings, are more heavy duty than those in conventional structures. Large windows flank the north-facing façade. These windows provide maximum daylight capture without generating excessive heat gain in the summer months. To prevent marked temperature increases, large overhangs were designed for the south façade. Energy is supplied by twenty-four photovoltaic panels that act as an energy-storage system.

ARCHITECT
Cass Smith, Sean Kennedy/CCS Architecture

COLLABORATORS
Kleinfelder (geo-technical); Gedding Engineering; (structural engineer); Sol Sierra Solar Energy System (solar consultant); Sonoma Mission Gardens (landscape); Boucher Bros (general contractor)

TOTAL SURFACE AREA
1,750 sq ft

COST
$350,000

PHOTOGRAPHY
© Brendan P. Macrae/Prime Lens Photography

This ecologically sustainable house makes use of building materials, such as structural slabs, low-emissivity glass in windows and skylights, low-VOC paints, and photovoltaic panels.

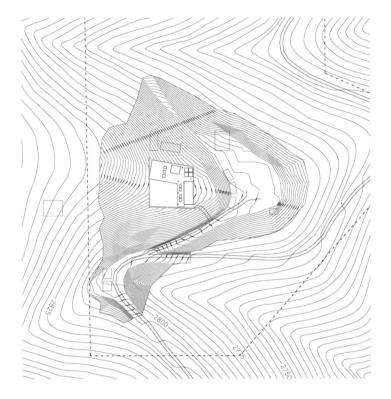

Site plan

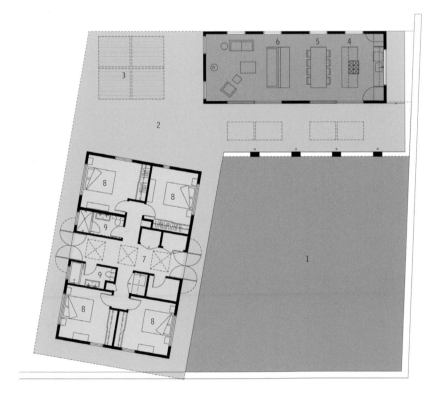

Live building
Sleep building

Plan

1. Courtyard
2. Breezeway
3. Lookout
4. Kitchen
5. Dining room
6. Living room
7. Gallery
8. Bedroom
9. Bathroom

BIG ROCK

Kangaroo Valley, NSW, Australia   2010

This residence is located in a rural area of Australia, only two hours away from Sydney. This project was designed to enable its owners to escape the city at least once a month, enjoy open-air activities, and reconnect with nature.

A key feature of the project is its fluid relationship between nature and architecture, as evidenced by the slightly suspended steel pavilion, large swimming pool with an extensive deck area, and paths that connect the house to the surrounding natural spaces. A small vantage point, located at the edge of a wooded part of the lot, is the perfect spot for moments of introspection. There is also an area that serves as a landing for boats.

ARCHITECT
Edward Szewczyk & Associates Architects

COLLABORATORS
D'Ambrosio Consulting (structural engineer); R & D Driver (builder); Shoalhaven Pools (pool contractor)

TOTAL SURFACE AREA
4,090.3 sq ft

PHOTOGRAPHY
© Michael Saggus, Edward Szewczyk

This house was made for weekend getaways. Every design element is intended to help the owners reconnect with nature, whether they are sitting in their living room or relaxing outdoors.

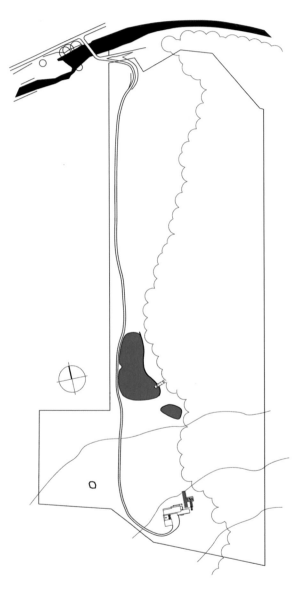

Site plan

North elevation

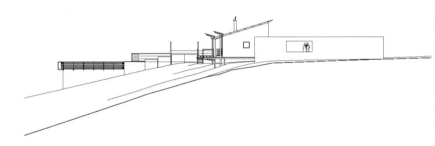

West elevation

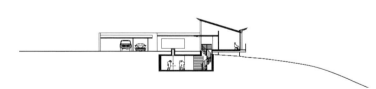

Section

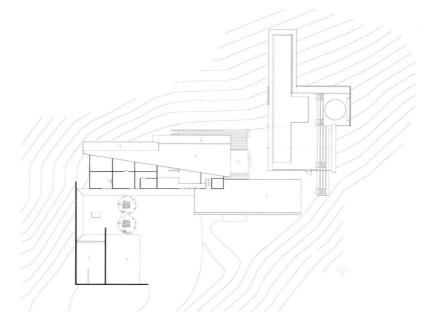

Roof plan

Ground floor plan

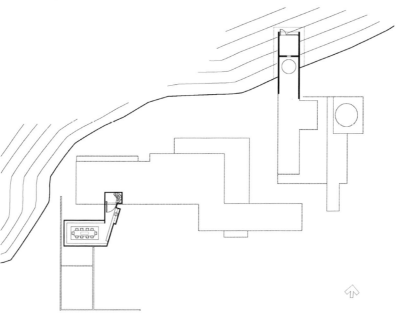

Basement plan

This house was made for weekend getaways. Every design element is intended to help the owners reconnect with nature, whether they are sitting in their living room or relaxing outdoors.

VILA NM

Catskills, NY, USA   2006

This summer house with spectacular views of woods and meadows is located two hours away from New York City. The sloping terrain of the site served as the base for this volume, which is in the form of a box that forks into two spaces. One of them follows the slope toward the north, while the other crowns the hill. This led to the creation of a covered parking area and internal layout through clearly defined changes in level.

The design has an interesting volume transition, the result of a series of five walls that revolve around a horizontal and vertical axis. In this way, the walls become the floor and the floor becomes the walls. This surface transition is repeated five times throughout the building. All the functional installations, such as bathroom, kitchen, and fireplace, are located in the vertical axis. The layout provided the option of removing outer walls from the project. The bedrooms, which require walls for privacy, are more limited, while the other areas have large glazed expanses.

In the public spaces, the kitchen and dining area on the first level also make use of this structure. Both are connected to the living area on the second level by a ramp, rising 1.5 m (5 ft) to a change in space and striking views of the valley. A similar ramp connects this level to the third floor, where the master bedroom and children's room are located.

ARCHITECT
UNStudio

COLLABORATORS
Olaf Gipser, Andrew Benn, Colette Parras, Jacco van Wengerden, Maria Eugenia Diaz, Jan Debelius, Martin Kuitert, Pablo Rica, Olga Vazquez-Ruano (design team); Roemer Pierik (consultant); Nicholas Pouder/Pouder Design Group, Jason Maciejevski/Maciejevski Landscaping (landscape design); Kenneth Arnoul/Swift Water Pools (pool construction)

TOTAL SURFACE AREA
2,690 sq ft

PHOTOGRAPHY
© UNStudio

136

The use of a characteristic feature enabled
cost savings to be made on the project without
sacrificing quality. The floor plan forks into two
spaces: one toward the north, and the other
crowning the hill, both with spectacular views.

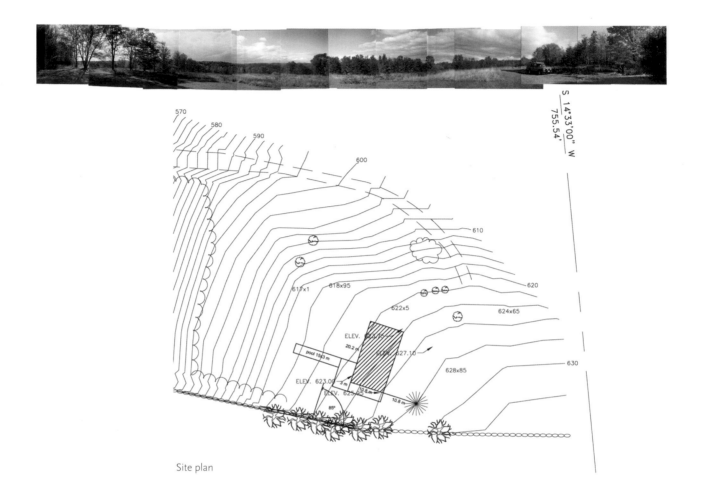

Site plan

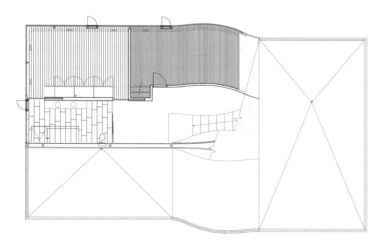

First floor plan

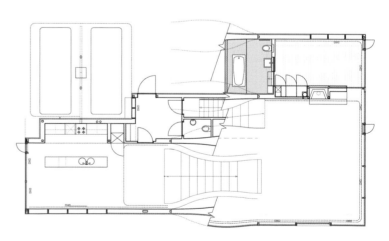

Ground floor plan

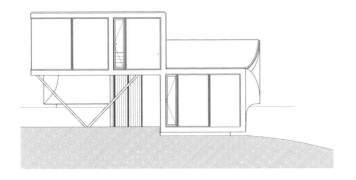

North elevation

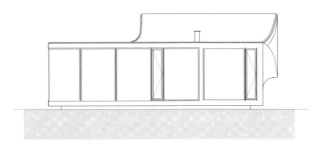

South elevation

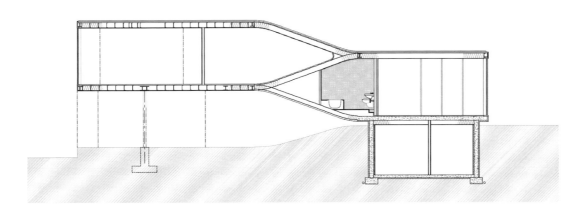

Section 1

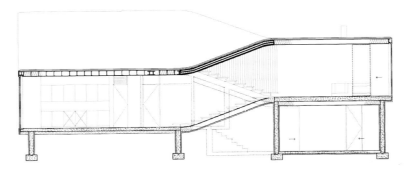

Section 2

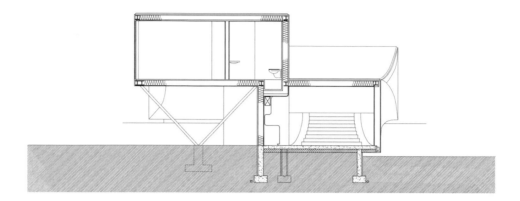

Section 3

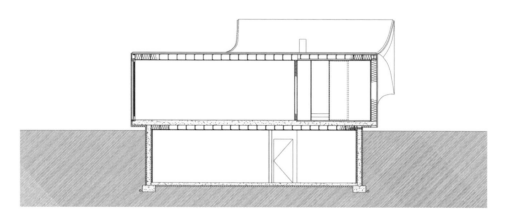

Section 4

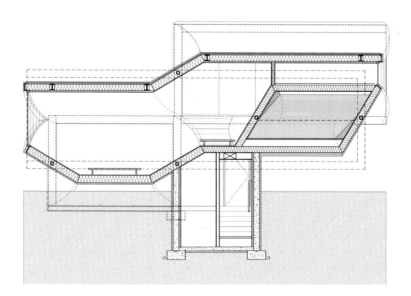

Section 5

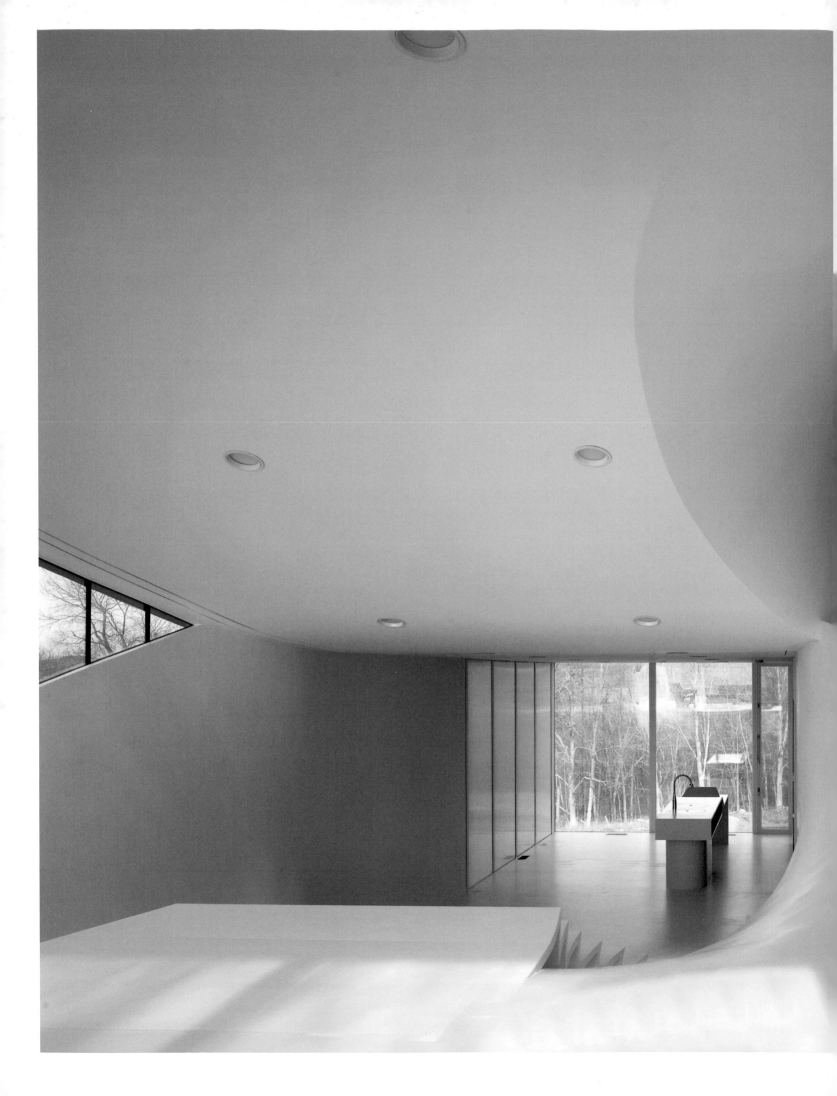

DESERT WING

Scottsdale, AZ, USA   2007

The Desert Wing House is located in the middle of Arizona's Sonoran Desert. The home is divided into two parts: a low-maintenance family unit for a couple who lives there throughout the year and a guest house.

The home is designed as a series of straight lines and was built from rammed earth and concrete blocks, two materials that can cope with the dryness and heat typical to the desert. The roof consists of planes that fold to collect rainwater, which is used to feed the surrounding vegetation. There were three main criteria that guided the choice of building materials: they had to be beautiful, low maintenance, and sourced locally. In keeping with this ideology, Arizona-mined copper clads the roof, and rammed earth walls, made from locally sourced materials, were built to echo the surrounding mountainous landscape. The result? A home in total harmony with its desert setting.

ARCHITECT
Brent Kendle/Kendle Design Collaborative

COLLABORATORS
Jack Wozniak (interior designer)

TOTAL SURFACE AREA
8,300 sq ft

PHOTOGRAPHY
© Rick Brazil

Desert Wing is located in the middle of the
Sonoran Desert and features locally sourced,
low-maintenance materials in its construction.

Context plan

Site plan

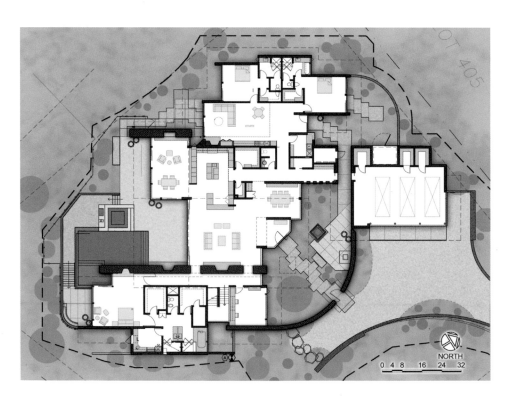

First floor plan

Earth tones dominate the color
scheme of the house's interior.

MONK'S SHADOW

Paradise Valley, AZ, USA 2009

The Monk's Shadow is a single-family home located in Paradise Valley, Arizona. The residence's design scheme revolves around the "Praying Monk," a famous rock formation in the area. The master bedroom looks out at the rock formation, and several other rooms in the house are framed with a similar view. The building site, while beautiful, was also difficult terrain, as reflected by a series of slopes. Several municipal ordinances also made some construction difficult.

The home is divided into three areas: the first area is for the parents, the second is for the children, and the third is for guests. The parents' area consists of the master bedroom suite and a family entertainment area. The children's section has bedrooms, a game room, and access to the swimming pool and one of the garages. The guests' area has a bedroom and private bathroom and a spare room used as a home office.

The building program includes a garden area featuring xeric landscaping, which favors desert species, such as cactus, together with a lawn. The roof was designed in the shape of a butterfly to use collected rainwater for watering. To further lessen the ecological imprint, the house is divided into high-energy efficiency zones for effective climate control.

ARCHITECT
Brent Kendle/Kendle Design Collaborative

COLLABORATORS
GBtwo Landscape Architecture Inc (landscape architect)

TOTAL SURFACE AREA
8,008.3 sq ft

PHOTOGRAPHY
© Rick Brazil

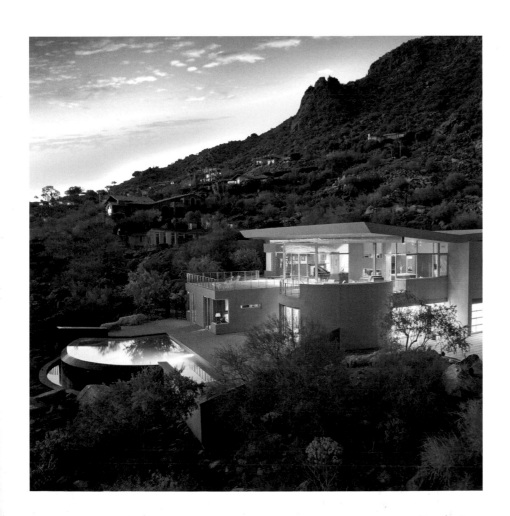

The garden features xeric landscaping. This gardening
style utilizes plant species that are well suited to
the scarcity of water and are native to the area.

Earth tones predominate throughout the house. This
color scheme blends with the natural surroundings.

BEACH HOUSE

Coastal Victoria, Australia   2010

This unusual beach house is located on the coast of the Australian state of Victoria. Referred to as the Beach House, it was designed to be a striking addition to an already beautiful landscape. According to its architects, this home was "anchored" to the site. The exterior features of the residence, such as the garden and swimming pool, also seem to be moored to the terrain.

With its abundant sequences of interior spatial folds, the building is designed as if it were an exercise in origami. The design is at once playful and intentional; the different spaces in the house are fluidly connected to one another.

The minimalist interior features glass and wood. The design of the house and the distribution of the different-sized windows afford impressive ocean views, no matter the room. The idea here is that the interior should welcome in the exterior, giving the owners and their guests the chance to feel connected to the beauty of the surrounding landscape without having to leave the sanctity of their home.

ARCHITECT
BKK Architects

COLLABORATORS
Julian Kosloff, Simon Knott, Tim Blank, Jane Caught, Michael Roper (project team); Overend Constructions (builder); Irwinconsult (structural engineer); Construction Planning and Economics (quantity surveyor)

TOTAL SURFACE AREA
3,756.6 sq ft

PHOTOGRAPHY
© Peter Bennetts

The Beach House was inspired by origami, a Japanese
technique of paper folding. The resulting design
features a large number of spatial folds in its interior.

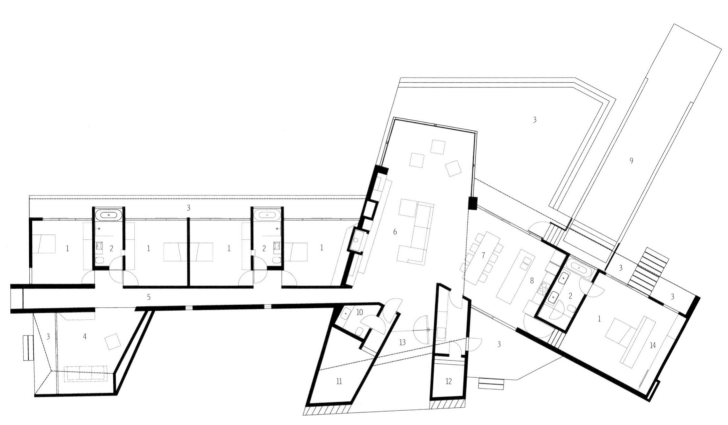

Plan

1. Bedroom
2. En suite bathroom
3. Deck
4. Retreat
5. Hall
6. Lounge
7. Dining room
8. Kitchen
9. Pool
10. Powder room
11. Laundry/wet room
12. Storage room
13. Entry
14. Walk-in wardrobe

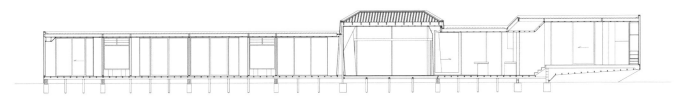

Longitudinal section

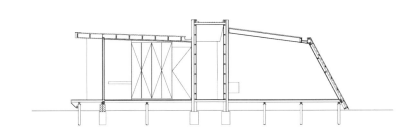

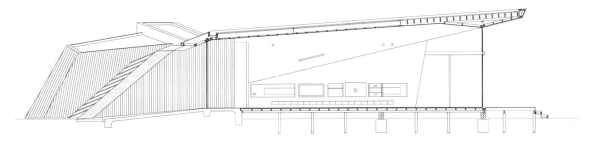

Cross sections

GREAT WALL OF WARBURTON

Warburton, VIC, Australia   2008

This Australian residence, known as the Great Wall of Warburton, is situated on an elevated site in a natural enclave of native bushland with hills lying to the north. This house continues a trend started by its architects, who use their designs to explore how interior spaces can engage with the surrounding landscape. To synthesize this unsubordinated and symbiotic relationship between the interior and the natural environment, a great wall was erected to anchor the house in the landscape.

Ceiling and floor levels were manipulated in the design to modulate this special relationship. Changes in level are strategically located to demarcate specific living areas. The narrowness of the floor plan, never wider than one room and hallway of normal dimensions, constantly drives the inhabitant to a closer association with the landscape. Each interior space becomes a framing device with subtle variations in the perspective offered by each room.

The interior of this narrow residence makes great use of wood, with stone walls combining masterfully with its surrounding hilly setting. The placement of windows along the entire façade offers harmonious views of the landscape.

ARCHITECT
BKK Architects

COLLABORATORS
Julian Kosloff, Simon Knott, Tim Blank, Lauren Dornau, Rory Hyde, George Huan, Michael Roper, Michael White, Adi Atic (project team); Overend Constructions (builder); Patrick Irwin/ Design Action Pty Ltd (engineer); Group II Building Surveyors (builder surveyor); Construction Planning and Economics (quantity surveyor)

TOTAL SURFACE AREA
3,466 sq ft

PHOTOGRAPHY
© Shannon McGrath

Located in the Australian municipality of Warburton, this house was christened the Great Wall of Warburton. The project seeks to become anchored harmoniously into the surrounding natural landscape. The predominant materials used in its construction were stone, wood, and glass.

Plan

1. Entry
2. Wet room
3. Studio
4. Bathroom
5. Bedroom
6. Deck
7. Spa/pool
8. Kitchen
9. Living room
10. Dining room
11. Hall

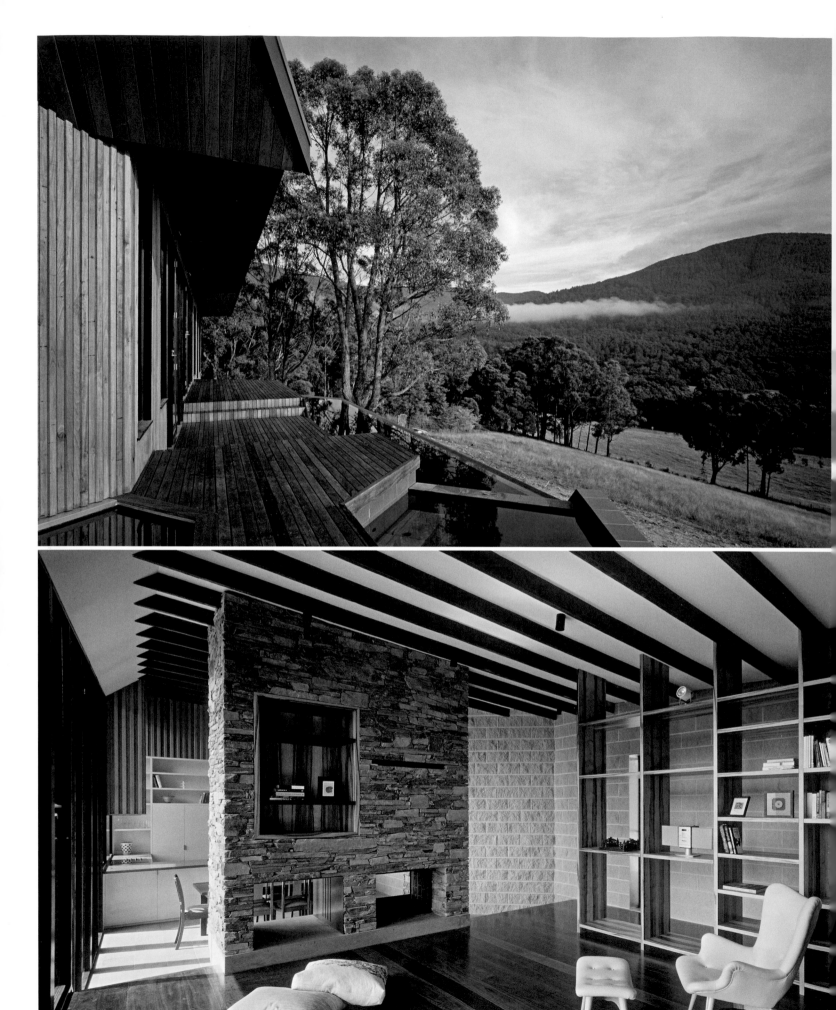

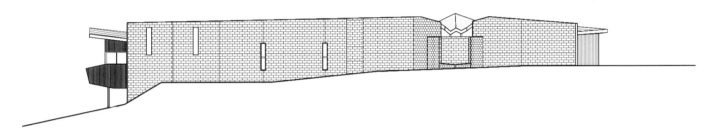

Southwest elevation

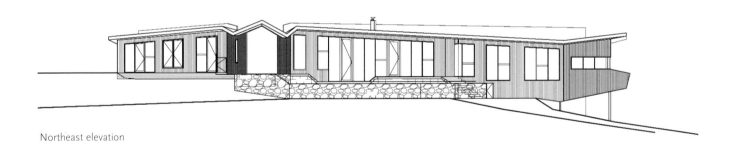

Northeast elevation

ROOSENDAAL RESIDENCE

Roosendaal, The Netherlands   2009

This home is located in Roosendaal, a town in the southern Netherlands. Its design is based on the idea of a house being a mass with several grooves. This concept does not allow for any overhangs, but it does allow for a second structure that will be a volume in itself. The goal of this building was to create a synthesis between interior and exterior spaces, with subtle transitions between the two.

The connection between the interior and the exterior spaces is made possible by several windows, which are deeply set in the façade. The house welcomes in tons of light; so much so, in fact, that it is the design's focal point. The living room was raised by 31.5 in (80 cm) to create a direct relation with the magnificent view. The different levels of the home interact by means of the central staircase, which has relatively small differences in height. Adjacent to the master bedroom is a terrace that leads to a split-level outside space. The form of this residence is a direct consequence of the terrain.

ARCHITECT
Ernst Havermans/Oomen Architecten

TOTAL SURFACE AREA
5,156 sq ft

PHOTOGRAPHY
© Filip Dujardin

This project was designed as a whole. The focal point
is the entry of light. Transitions between interior and
exterior are embodied in windows deeply set in the
façade that allow light flow to dominate over all.

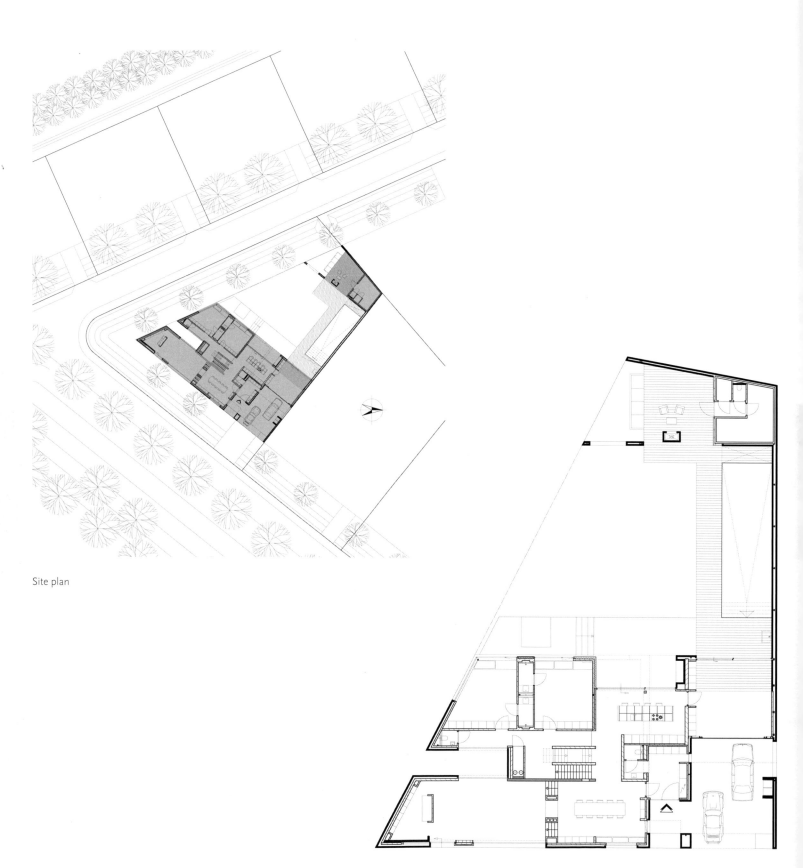

Site plan

Plan

VG RESIDENCE

Pacific Palisades, CA, USA   2010

This house is located on a site that is as beautiful as it is uneven. In order to achieve the best use of the difficult terrain, the residence was designed in a way so it didn't stand out from the surrounding landscape, but instead simply proposed a new way of seeing it.

The design revolves around retaining walls, built to provide strength and to withstand natural forces. The residence stands on a rocky terrain that is raised toward the east and falls away in all other directions. In fact, the natural rock wall on the east side serves as a safeguard for the entire project. There are two structures: the main residence and a guest house. In order to make full use of the building area, a patio was built outside the main house. This patio features a large infinity pool that stretches to the edge of the cliff. A path leads from the pool to a private fitness room. The house also features a roof terrace with panoramic views of the coast.

ARCHITECT
Eric Rosen Architects

COLLABORATORS
Eric Rosen (principal); Lesley Graham (project manager); David Milner, Braden LeMaster, Joseph Tran (project team); David Lau/David H. Lau & Associates Inc (structural engineer); Richard Rybak/ Rybak Geotechnical Inc (geotechnical engineer); David Daniels, Electronic System Consultants (AV consultant); Rotondi Construction (general contractor)

TOTAL SURFACE AREA
5,500 sq ft

PHOTOGRAPHY
© Erich Koyama

The home features a number of areas devoted to leisure and amusement. The roof terrace, for example, offers singular panoramic views of the surrounding area, the pool, and the fitness room.

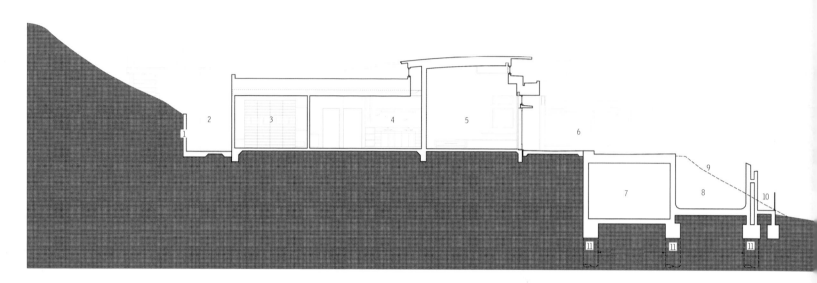

Section A-A

1.	Retaining wall	7.	Fitness room
2.	Back patio	8.	Pool
3.	Master closet	9.	Line of natural grade
4.	Master bathroom	10.	Hidden walkway
5.	Master bedroom	11.	Deepened footings
6.	Master bedroom patio		

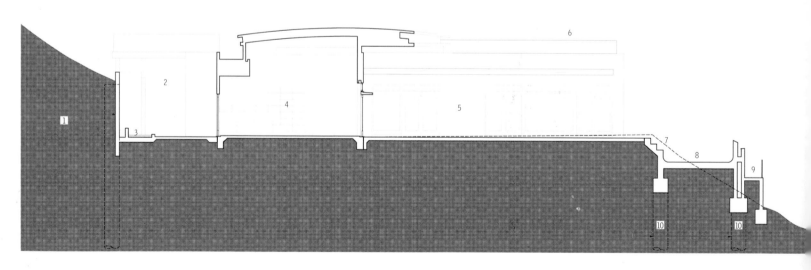

Section B-B

1.	Retaining wall	6.	Deck roof
2.	Back patio	7.	Line of natural grade
3.	Fountain	8.	Pool
4.	Studio	9.	Hidden walkway
5.	Courtyard	10.	Deepened footings

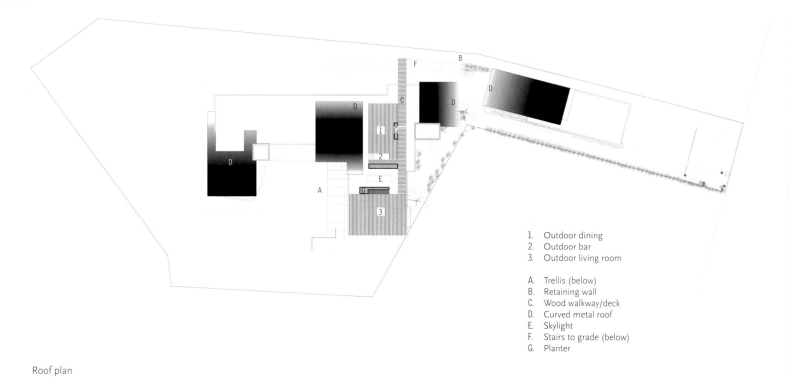

Roof plan

1. Outdoor dining
2. Outdoor bar
3. Outdoor living room

A. Trellis (below)
B. Retaining wall
C. Wood walkway/deck
D. Curved metal roof
E. Skylight
F. Stairs to grade (below)
G. Planter

Plan

1. Garage
2. Guest bathroom
3. Guest room
4. Entry
5. Powder room 1
6. Closet
7. Bar
8. Living room
9. Dining room
10. Kitchen
11. Breakfast nook
12. Back entry
13. Pantry
14. Media room
15. Laundry/utility room

16. Maid's bathroom
17. Maid's room
18. Studio
19. Bedroom
20. Bathroom
21. Master bedroom
22. Master bathroom
23. Master closet
24. Pool
25. Spa
26. Barbecue
27. Fitness room (below)
28. Master bedroom patio
29. Lower patio
30. Hidden walkway

31. Living room patio
32. Courtyard
33. Loggia
34. Back patio/fountain
35. Patio/garden
36. Entry walkway
37. Driveway

A. Trellis (above)
B. Retaining wall
C. Bridge to roof deck (above)
D. Fountain
E. Stairs to roof deck

HOUSE IN MARTINHAL
Martinhal, Portugal   2007

This beach house is situated in the heart of the Portuguese region of the Algarve, a town famous for having been the location of Prince Henry the Navigator's seafaring school during Portugal's Age of Discoveries. Today, however, the waters that bathe the Sagres coast are famous for their perfect windsurfing conditions.

Both the building site and the building itself were subject to different regulations. This meant that the project had to respect minimum distances to the edges and other specifications regarding access and volume. The structure is white with a flat roof, typical to the area, and used for drying fruit and fish. The house is divided into different volumes. The largest, in length and height, is located on the northern part of the site, protecting the inner marble courtyard from the strong winds that are typical of the region. The bedrooms are located in an L-shaped layout, which affords greater privacy to occupants. The house also has a certain Arab influence, with a courtyard articulating the different spaces.

ARCHITECT
Nuno Mateus, José Mateus/ARX
Portugal Arquitectos

COLLABORATORS
SAFRE Projectos e Estudos de
Engenharia Lda. (structure engineering)

TOTAL SURFACE AREA
3,444.5 sq ft

PHOTOGRAPHY
© ARX Portugal Arquitectos,
FG + SG Fotografía de Arquitectura

The architecture studio combined several architectural typologies in the design of this home: the traditional "Portuguese home" in the main structure, Arabic influences in the main courtyard and flat, white roofs typical of the architecture in the area.

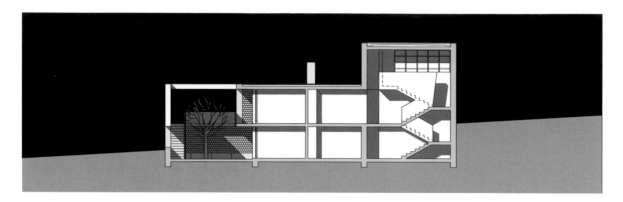

Cross section

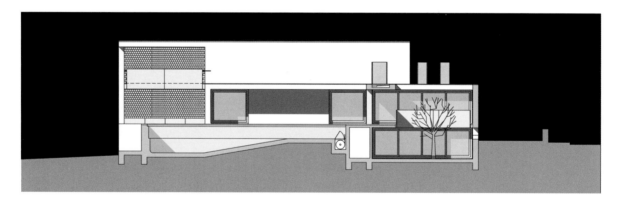

Longitudinal section

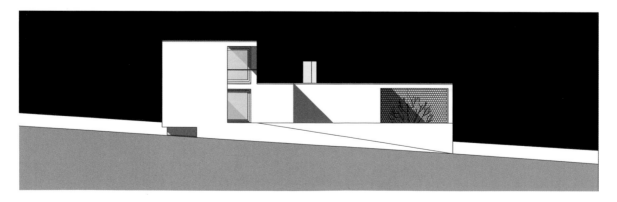

South elevation

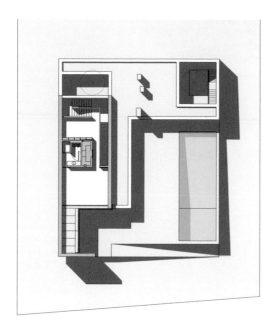

First floor plan

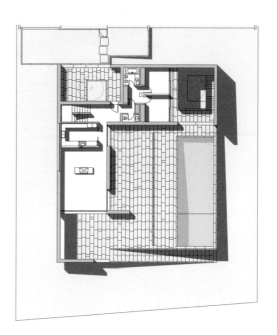

Ground floor plan

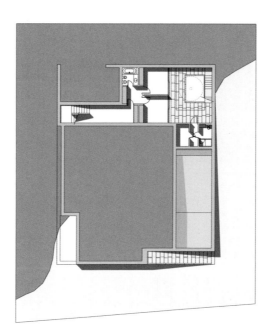

Basement plan

VILLA 1

Ede, The Netherlands   2008

Located in a Dutch pine forest, this home is laid out over a site that offers beautiful views while being exposed to abundant daylight. The design included an orientation to enhance and maximize the panorama and light penetration. In compliance with local planning rules, half of the building was sunk into the ground. The result was a dichotomy in the spatial experience of the residence: a glass box above the ground concentrates most of the furnished spaces, leaving a basement area underground. The unique floor plan is Y-shaped, with three clearly differentiated wings.

The north wing is for studying, working, and playing music. The east-south-west wing is for cooking and eating, while the south-north wing is for resting and painting. The wings meet in a central area at the heart of the home. This space serves as a foyer, dining room, bar, and place for listening to music. On the south and east sides, two large sunny terraces create restful interior spaces. The Y-shaped basement is clearly functional. One wing is the master bedroom, another is a garage, while the third is a guestroom. A courtyard provides the guest area with daylight.

Each wing is laid out centrifugally, but everything is concentrated in the central core. All services and structural elements are concealed in a unit, which in turn divides the core into different areas in a completely glazed space. Free transit is achieved by this. It is possible to enjoy a walk 492 ft (150 m) through all the different landscape-immersed rooms.

ARCHITECT
Powerhouse Company

COLLABORATORS
Nanne de Ru (partner in charge); Charles Bessard, Alexander Sverdlov (design); Nolly Vos, Wouter Hermanns, Anne Luetkenhues, Bjørn Andreassen, Joe Matthiessen (project team); Gilbert van der Lee/BREED ID (structural engineering); Valleibouw BV Veenendaal (contractor); Smeulders IG (interior contractor); LS2, Bert Roseboom, BEDA electro (lighting consultants)

TOTAL SURFACE AREA
5,167 sq ft

PHOTOGRAPHY
© Powerhouse Company

Industrial building techniques were employed. The basement is concrete. The roof is a complex steel structure. The library is also made of solid steel panels and serves as a frame to keep the roof steady.

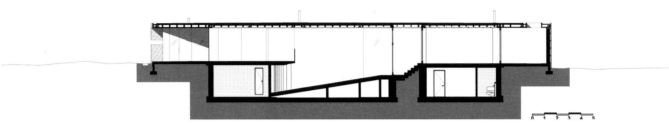

Section A-A

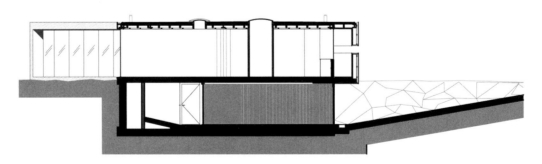

Section C-C

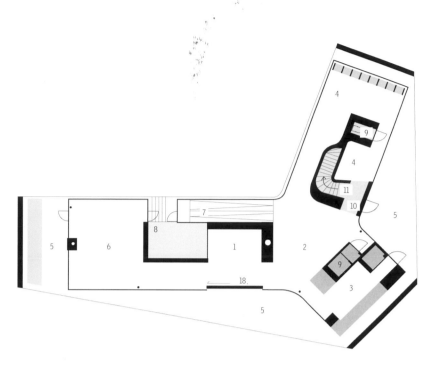

Ground floor plan

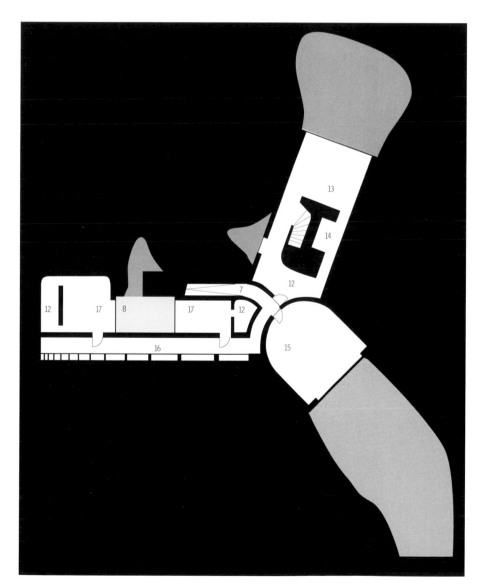

Basement plan

1. Living room
2. Hall
3. Kitchen
4. Studio
5. Terrace
6. Atelier
7. Ramp
8. Patio
9. Bathroom
10. Entry
11. Staircase
12. Bathroom
13. Bedroom
14. Walk-in closet
15. Garage
16. Storage corridor
17. Guestroom
18. Gimp room

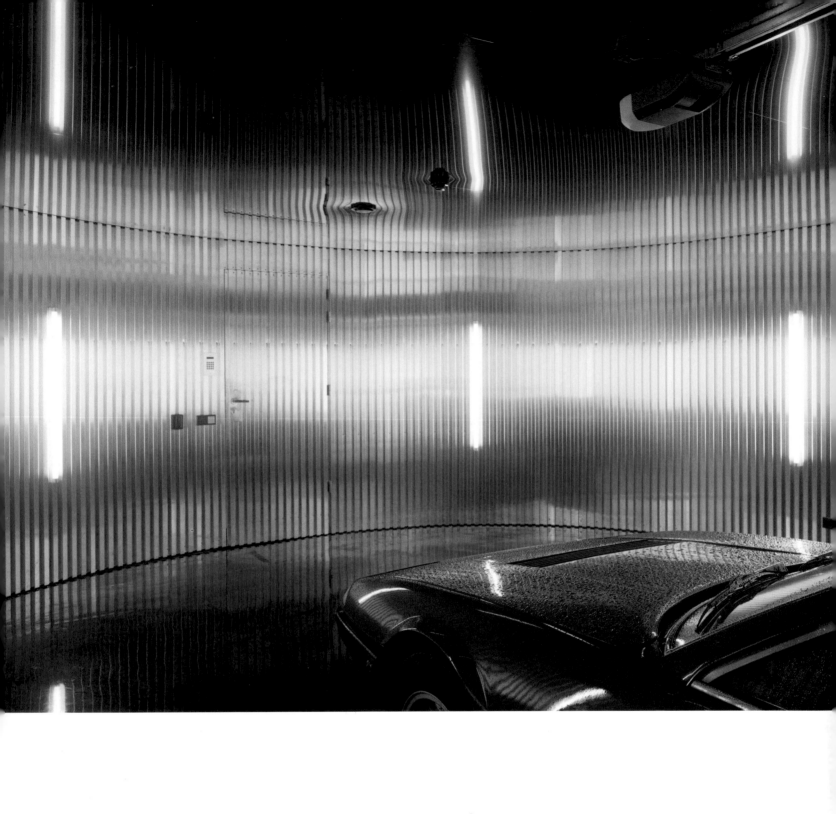

TREEHOUSE

Seattle, WA, USA   2009

This project is located in a wooded area of Seattle, Washington, on a difficult-to-reach sloping site. The challenging program was achieved for the creation of a single-family home high among the trees.

The design was aimed toward the long-term minimization of environmental impacts on the surroundings, cost-effective building, and the efficient use of existing resources. It also aspired to enhance the view, light, and the setting—the most valuable aspects of the project—despite the difficult terrain, and to accentuate the sensation of living in the treetops.

Due to the topography, steel structures were used to support the house above the slope and between the trees. The existing gradient was also retained in order to preserve the forest's natural drainage system. The building incorporated sustainable design criteria. Among them was that of reducing impact on the environment through the design, in addition to contemplating long-term uses and energy costs. Hydraulic radiators were employed for the heating system and use was made of recycled furniture.

The interior features a double-height void that gives the impression of being in a large house. Openings accentuate the connection with the site, the treetops, and the sky. Daylight enters from above through a skylight into the core of the home, an expanse connecting the interior spaces.

ARCHITECT
SHED Architecture & Design

TOTAL SURFACE AREA
1,647 sq ft

PHOTOGRAPHY
© SHED Architecture & Design

Despite the challenges posed by the terrain, this project managed to enhance its most valuable aspects—view, light, and the setting—adding to the wonderful experience of living in the treetops.

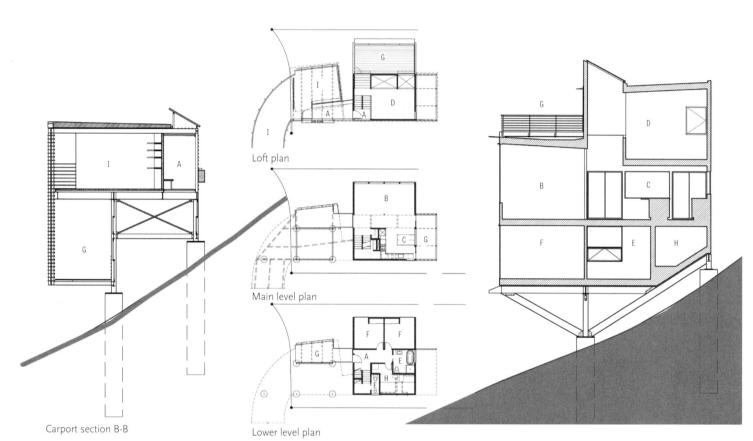

Carport section B-B

Loft plan

Main level plan

Lower level plan

House section B-B

A. Entry
B. Living/dining room
C. Kitchen
D. Loft/office
E. Bathroom
F. Bedroom
G. Deck
H. Laundry/storage room
I. Carport/driveway

HOUSE IN CARABBIA

Carabbia, Switzerland   2007

Located in the village of Carabbia, a beautiful valley on the western side of Mount San Salvatore in the Swiss canton of Ticino, this house is characterized by geometric structures that delimit an organized development of spaces. The outstanding feature of this project is the interior-interior and interior-exterior spatial relationship, which aims to increase the living area.

It is pared down square geometry, where spaces meet the slope and extend in a spiral movement that constantly changes the perception of space and its relation with the exterior, offering privileged views of the beautiful countryside.

This small house measures 43 × 43 ft (13 × 13 m), and is based on a series of condensed experiences in a continuous space, which provides a feeling of protection. The steeply sloped roof continues the inclination of the terrain and is the reaction of the building to the mountainside, proposing a language that is more organic than urban. The design is characterized by a slope of approximately 30° toward the west. The three main stories of the house are placed to correspond with their height level on the ground. The view on entry takes in the entire interior space, together with the connected exterior space. This enhances the perception of size, while the house is actually quite small: a built surface area of approximately 1,830 sq ft (170 m²), although the perception is that of 3,230 sq ft (300 m²). The entrance to the house is at mezzanine level between the upper and intermediate floors, where the kitchen and dining areas are located. The first floor, the lowest level of the house, is where the three bedrooms are located. All the levels are interconnected.

ARCHITECT
Davide Macullo, Marco Strozzi/Davide Macullo Architects

CLIENT
Botta family

COLLABORATORS
Laura Perolini, Michele Alberio (design team); Luigi Pellegrinelli/Ideal Ingegno SA (engineering); Franco Semini (physical engineering); DL Direzione Lavori (project manager)

TOTAL SURFACE AREA
1,830 sq ft

PHOTOGRAPHY
© Pino Musi, Enrico Cano

Research was made into the perception of
spaces, leading to the idea that space can be
understood by spending time in it. In addition
to form and design, time is a useful tool in
the creative stage of designing a space.

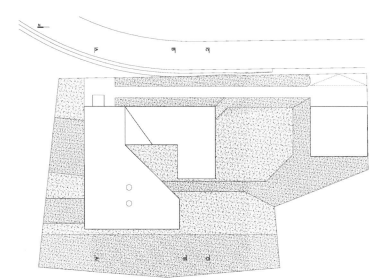

Roof plan

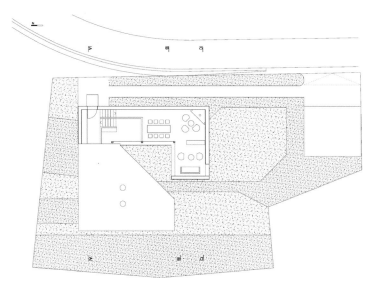

Living/dining room level plan

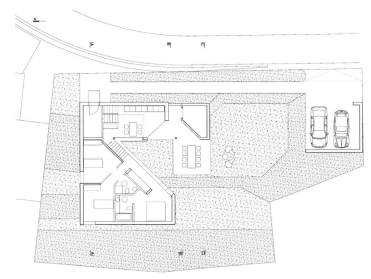

Entry/bedroom level plan

KING RESIDENCE

Santa Monica, CA, USA   2008

This house was designed for the typical resident family of Sunset Park in Santa Monica, California. This neighborhood was originally built to house workers during the Second World War. One mile from the beach, it occupies a corner site of 14,000 sq ft (1,310 m) on a gentle slope. This project rejects the typical strategy involved in planning standard houses, with a public garden in front and a private yard at the back. Here, the opposite orientation is given so that the main areas of the house face the yard.

The structure itself consists of a series of vertical and horizontal planes. The dining room roof and eaves point downward and follow the gently sloping site.

The house's qualities enable it to fit well into its environment. A void is created on the street instead of a volume. The residence is situated at the rear of the lot, without overwhelming the neighborhood. The design speaks of good manners and generosity. These qualities are enhanced by the composition of overlapping planes and layers, which break from the mass and project a sense of permeability; one can see directly through the house from the street.

ARCHITECT
John Friedman Alice Kimm Architects

COLLABORATORS
John Friedman, Alice Kimm (principals-in-charge); Anthony Bonomo/Bonomo Development (general contractor)

TOTAL SURFACE AREA
4,300 sq ft

PHOTOGRAPHY
© Benny Chan/Fotoworks

Inside and out, the design communicates a
serious yet casual feel. It creates the conditions
for a flexible lifestyle and makes use of a
refined choice of materials and details.

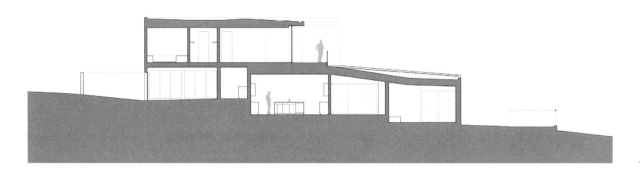

Section A

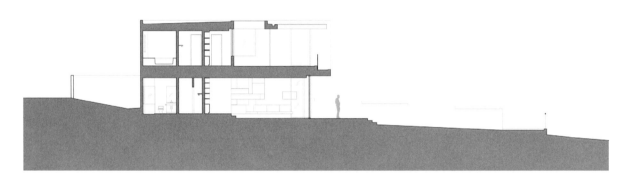

Section B

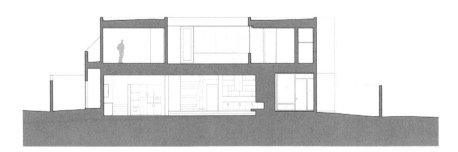

Section C

235

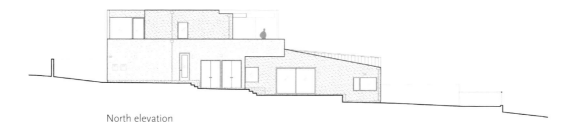

North elevation

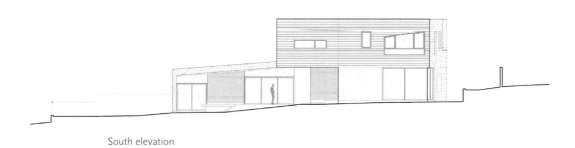

South elevation

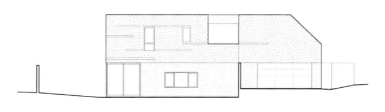

West elevation

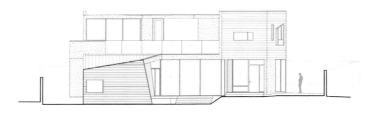

East elevation

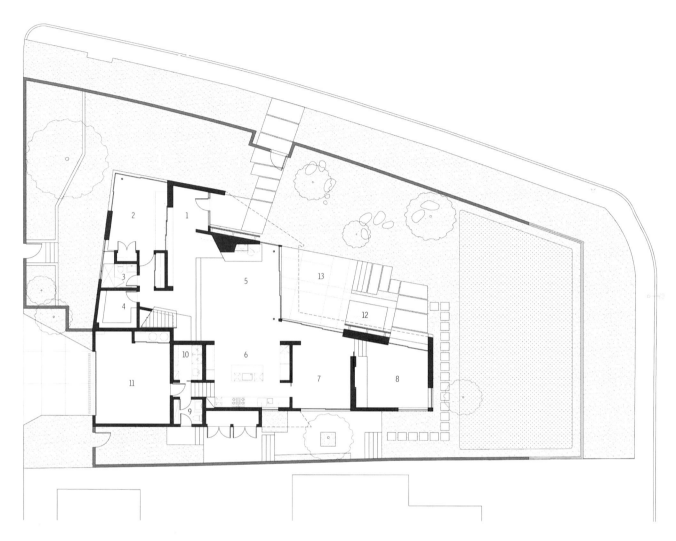

Ground floor plan

1. Foyer
2. Office
3. Bathroom
4. Wine cellar
5. Living room
6. Kitchen
7. Dining room
8. Hang-out room
9. Powder room
10. Laundry room
11. Garage
12. Fountain
13. Patio

SKYLINE RESIDENCE

Los Angeles, CA, USA   2007

The Skyline Residence is a single-family home that sits high in California's Hollywood Hills. This home posed a double challenge for the architects. Firstly, the site was very narrow—it is bordered by steep hillsides. Secondly, there were budget constraints. For these reasons, the team developed a concept they called Carbon Neutral Economics, which guided the architectural process. In an effort to reduce carbon emissions from transport and imports, the team favored the use of locally manufactured goods. The soil excavated from the site was reused, as was low-emissivity glass, which was also made in California. The team utilized recycled framing and flooring from nearby demolition sites.

The residence features a main house and a guest house, both of which were built to a series of lighting parameters that influenced the layout. Those parameters included protection from direct daylight, the creation of optimum viewing angles, and maximum exposure to natural light. Every room has at least one fully glazed wall and an orientation that offers amazing views of either Central Los Angeles or the San Fernando Valley. For the space between the main house and the guest house, the team created a casual leisure area, with one wall doubling as a movie screen.

ARCHITECT
Belzberg Architects

COLLABORATORS
Hagy Belzberg (principal); Erik Sollom, Manish Desai (project managers); Bill Bowen (construction manager); Barry Gartin, Brock DeSmit, Carina Bien Willner, Dan Rentsch, David Cheung, Eric Stimmel, Erin McCook, Ryan Thomas (project team); Dan Echeto (structural engineer); Nicholas Budd Dutton Architects (landscape architects)

TOTAL SURFACE AREA
5,800 sq ft

PHOTOGRAPHY
© Benny Chan/Fotoworks

Due to the uneven terrain, it was necessary to make use of the surrounding scrub to prevent some areas of relatively unstable soil from sliding away.

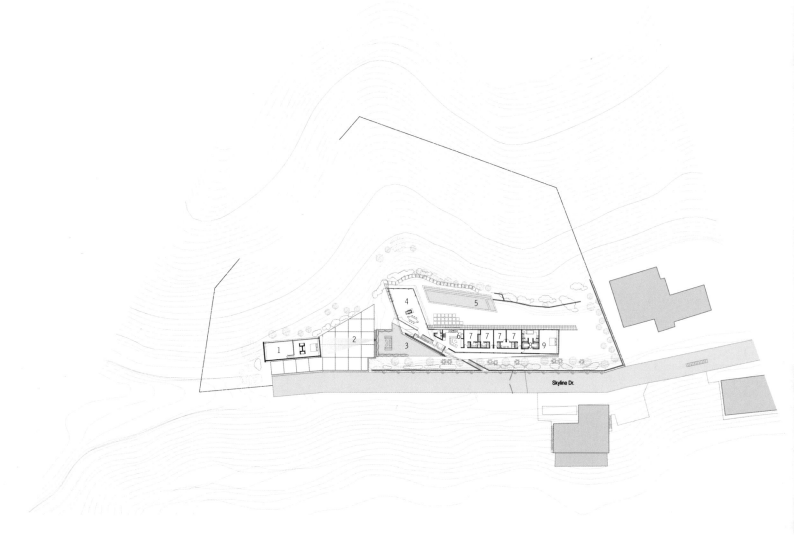

Site plan

1. Guest house/carport (2 levels)
2. Turnaround driveway/outdoor movie seating
3. Outdoor movie deck/garage (below)
4. Living/dining room
5. Infinity edge pool
6. Kitchen
7. Bedrooms
8. Master bathroom
9. Master bedroom

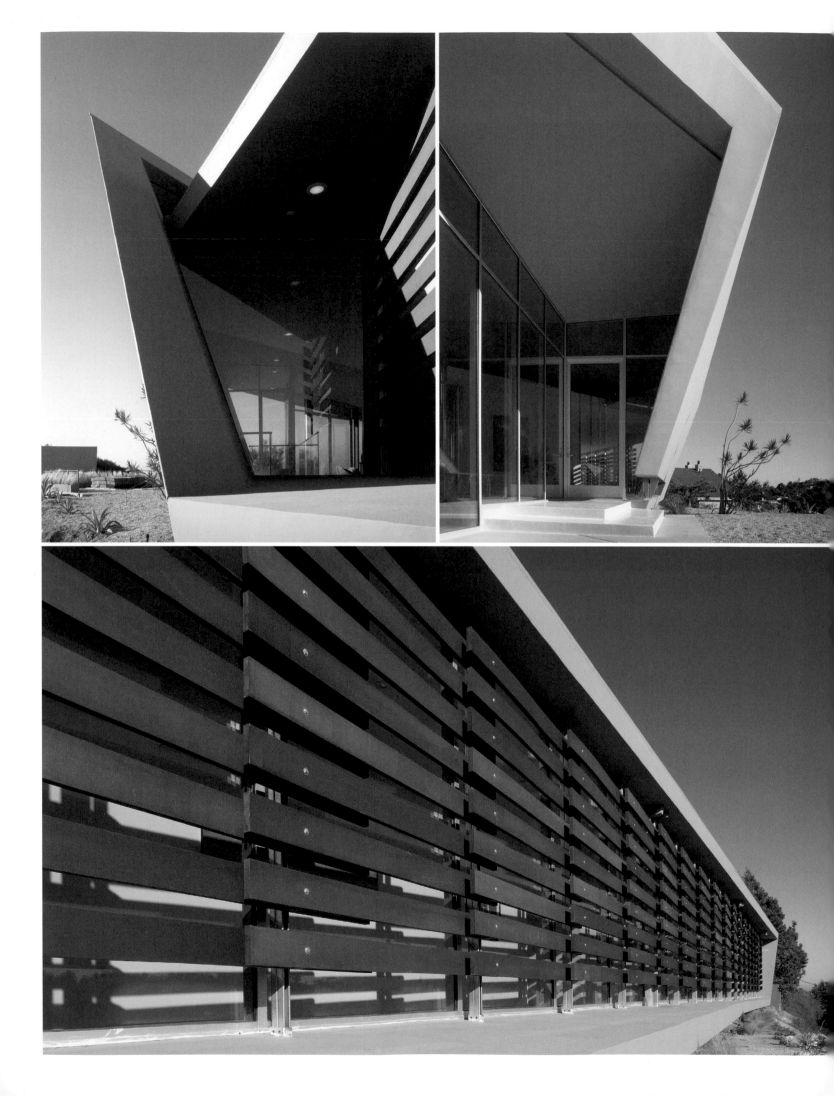

Not only does the residence offer dramatic views, it also welcomes in tons of natural light. Every space is utilized to full effect, including the space between the two houses, which features an outdoor movie theater.

PARATY HOUSE

Paraty, Brazil   2009

This beach house is located on one of the 365 Brazilian islands dotting the bay off the town of Paraty, between São Paulo and Rio de Janeiro. This residence shows great structural ingenuity while finding its balance in the layout of the terrain. It consists of two concrete boxes with a gallery set on a hillside. The house projects outward from the hill, and seemingly hovers over the beach with a cantilevered projection of 26 ft (8 m). The residents reach the house by boat. A metal bridge extends over a glass-lined reflecting pool at the entrance of the house. This bridge connects to stairs that lead into the house's lower volume, which contains the living area, kitchen, and service area. The interior of the house is decorated with classic twentieth-century designer furniture. The stairs rise up to connect the upper volume of the house, containing the bedrooms. In front, retractile panels made from eucalyptus sticks protect the rooms from the sun. The spaces closer to the hill have internal courtyards with zenithal lighting. Multiple terraces offer a variety of vantage points to take in majestic views of the surrounding countryside and ocean.

ARCHITECT
Marcio Kogan

COLLABORATORS
Marcio Kogan, Suzana Glogowski (architects); Diana Radomysler, Carolina Castroviejo (interior designers); Beatriz Meyer, Eduardo Chalabi, Eduardo Glycerio, Gabriel Kogan, Lair Reis, Luciana Antunes, Maria Cristina Motta, Mariana Simas, Oswaldo Pessano, Renata Furlanetto, Samanta Cafardo (project team)

TOTAL SURFACE AREA
9,041.7 sq ft

PHOTOGRAPHY
© Nelson Kon

The sections show how volumes inserted in the mountains are cantilevered outward to a distance of 26 ft (8 m). The home has been designed to look like a veranda overlooking the sea.

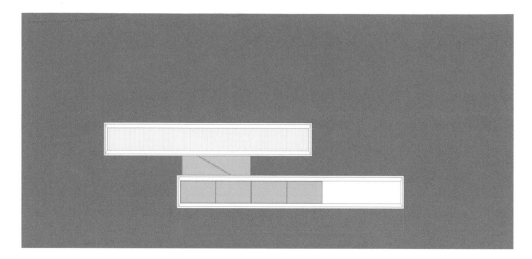

Front view

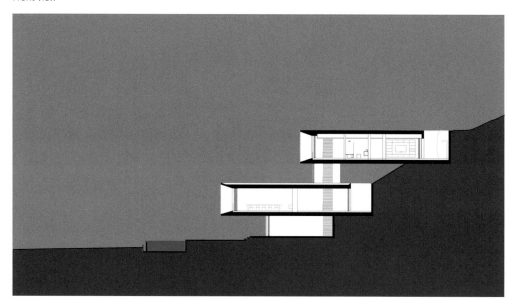

Section B

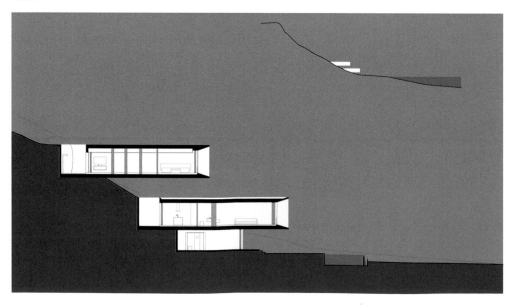

Landscape insertion/section A

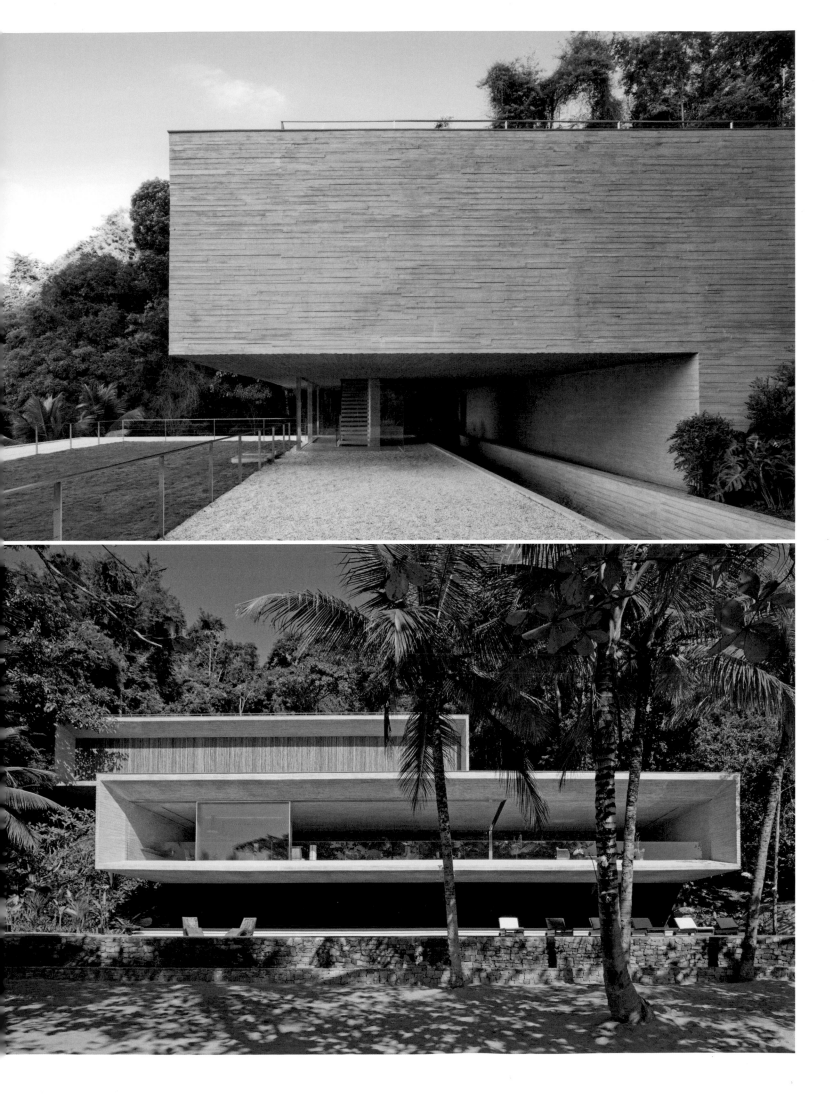

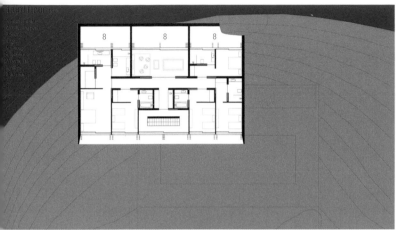

Third floor plan

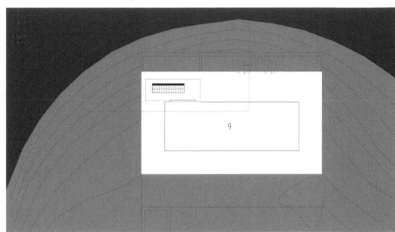

Second floor plan

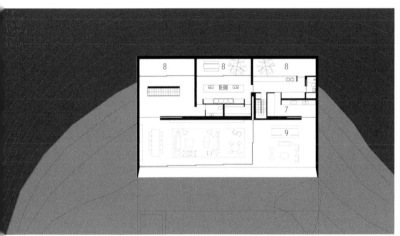

irst floor plan

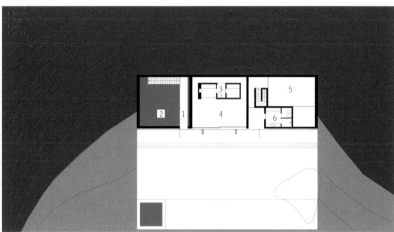

Ground floor plan

1. Main entrance
2. Reflecting pool
3. Sauna
4. Gym
5. Storage room
6. Laundry room
7. Barbecue
8. Patio
9. Terrace

ORQUÍDEA HOUSE

Pilar, Argentina   2008

To design this home, the team referenced one of the owners' favorite hobbies: growing orchids. The architects envisioned the home as a concrete and glass orchid, and designed a structure comprised of roots, stem, and flower. The root area, closest to the street, contains the garage and entrance. The stem, a connecting area between the root and the flower, houses part of the owners' private art collection. The flower area contains different living areas, arranged as petals and a bulb. Each of these spaces fulfills a different function and is connected by a central space featuring a skylight that enables daylight to reach each of the parts making up the bulb. The bulb is the place where each petal is connected with the upper and lower levels of the house. The layout made it possible to group public areas on the lower level and private spaces on the upper floor. Each space was given an orientation that was most suitable to take advantage of daylight entering the house. This produced significant energy savings. Air chambers were built into walls, ceilings, and joinery. This, together with the placement of folding windows on the first floor, adds to the responsible use of natural resources.

ARCHITECT
Andrés Remy Arquitectos

COLLABORATORS
Andrés Remy, Hernán Pardillos, Carlos Arellano, Lucila López, Paula Mancini, Julieta Rafel (design team); Lilian Kandus, Coral Banegas, Gisela Colombo, Diego Siddi, Martín Delatorre, Juan Etala, Sebastián Remy

TOTAL SURFACE AREA
5,005 sq ft

PHOTOGRAPHY
© Alejandro Peral

The Orquídea House is as environmentally sound
as it is cutting-edge. Over the years, its shape and
space can adapt to fit the owners' needs and wants.

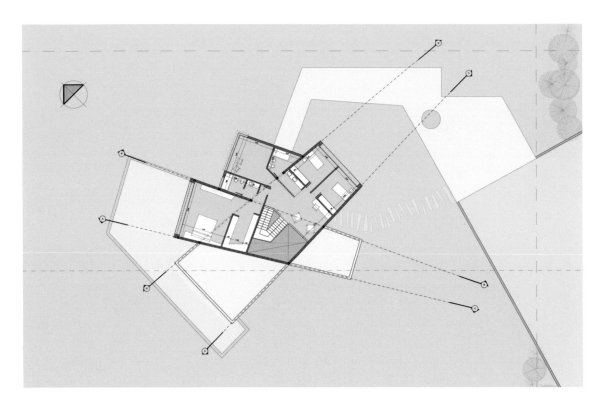

First floor plan

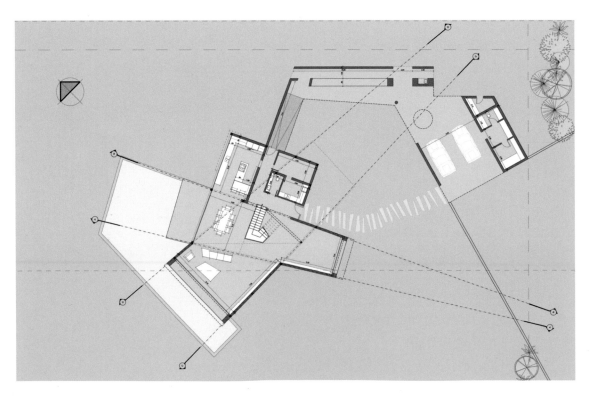

Ground floor plan

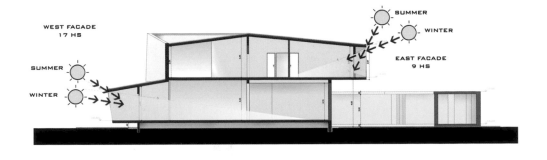

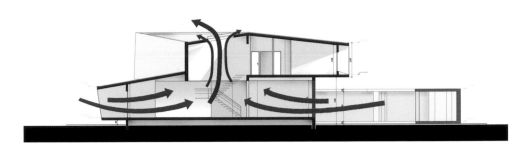

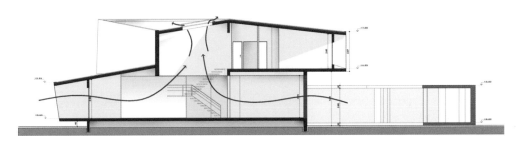

Bioclimatic schemes

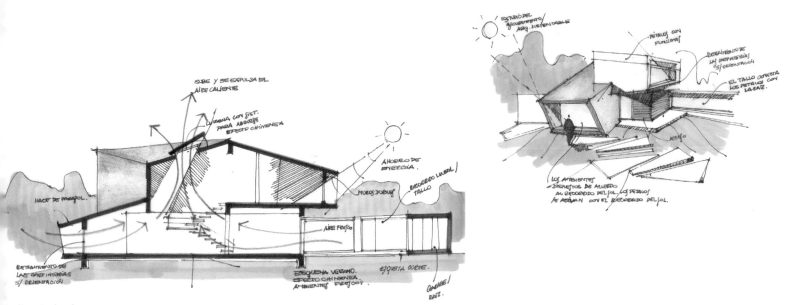

ioclimatic sketches

OPEN HOUSE

Hollywood Hills, CA, USA   2007

Located on a hill, this residence stands out as a solid sculptural form developed on a large spatial scale. The logic of its architecture was developed directly from the conditions of the terrain: the building fits the natural contours, and the interior spaces are stretched to embrace nature. Nature is extended through the home. Located on a steeply sloping site with a challenging terrain, this project has a design that attempts to integrate the home into its natural setting and also with the city it overlooks. Perpendicular steel beams were positioned toward and in the hillside to create the hanging structure at the front of the building. The result is the large terraces that extend the second level out over the hill.

The rear, front, and sides of the house are open to blur the limits between inside and out, and to connect internal spaces with the gardens and terraces on the three levels. This design allows the house to have unobstructed panoramic views over the city. The deep overhangs also serve to protect the double-glazed windows from the sun and become increasingly larger as the building climbs up the contours of the hillside. There are few finishes, but they are applied in such a variety of ways that they provide a feeling of a continuous space, with a seamless transition from outside to inside. The fireplace is made from dry stacked granite, which continues as a vertical structural element from the living area on the second level toward the third floor.

ARCHITECT
XTEN Architecture

CLIENT
Randolph Duke

COLLABORATORS
Peddicord Construction
(general contractor)

TOTAL SURFACE AREA
5,000 sq ft

PHOTOGRAPHY
© Art Gray Photography

Glass is the predominant material on walls. Forty-four sliding floor-to-ceiling panels were used. Each side of the house opens to capture the prevailing breezes and to ventilate interior spaces.

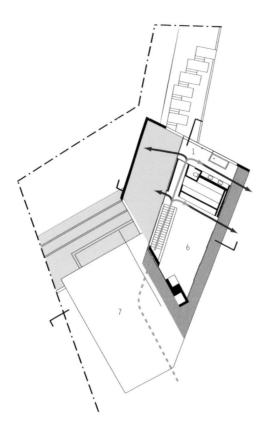

Second floor plan

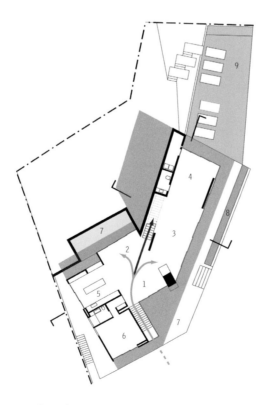

First floor plan

Xeriscape garden
Artificial turf
Overhangs

← Passive ventilation

1. Living room
2. Dining room
3. Den
4. Media room
5. Kitchen
6. Bedroom
7. Terrace
8. Pool
9. Garden

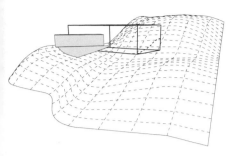
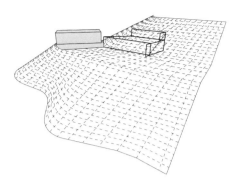
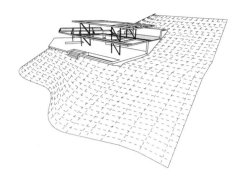

Diagrams

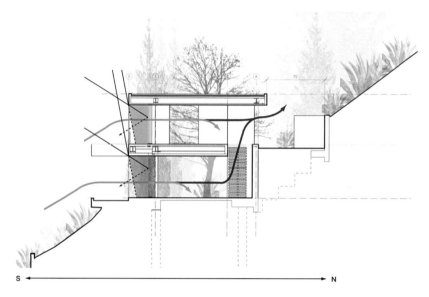

S ← → N

Section and diagram

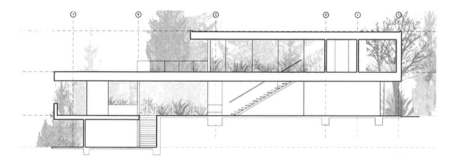

Longitudinal section

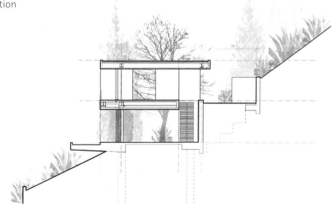

Cross section

BEACH HOUSE ON A HILL

Lima, Peru   2006

Located 62 miles (100 km) south of Lima, the capital of Peru, this beach house stands on a small hill along a stretch of coastline surrounded by desert. The house's design is unique due to its south-facing orientation and hilltop placement. While one side of the house offers a spectacular view of the Andes, the other is a vantage point for views of picturesque coastal villages and the sea. Floor-to-ceiling windows allow abundant natural daylight to fall into the rooms, and balconies further enhance the design. A water feature graces one side of the house, and gives the illusion that the building is floating. The house itself stands on a large vertical pedestal that forms the base for two planes. The extension of both planes forms an area of considerable dimensions that houses a public area consisting of kitchen and living/dining area.

ARCHITECT
Javier Artadi/Artadi Arquitectos

TOTAL SURFACE AREA
3,512 sq ft

PHOTOGRAPHY
© Alfio Garozzo

The greatest appeal of this beach house is that its
construction features make it a sight in itself. Its
singular location, nestled in Peru, provides the
perfect backdrop for a myriad of relaxing views.

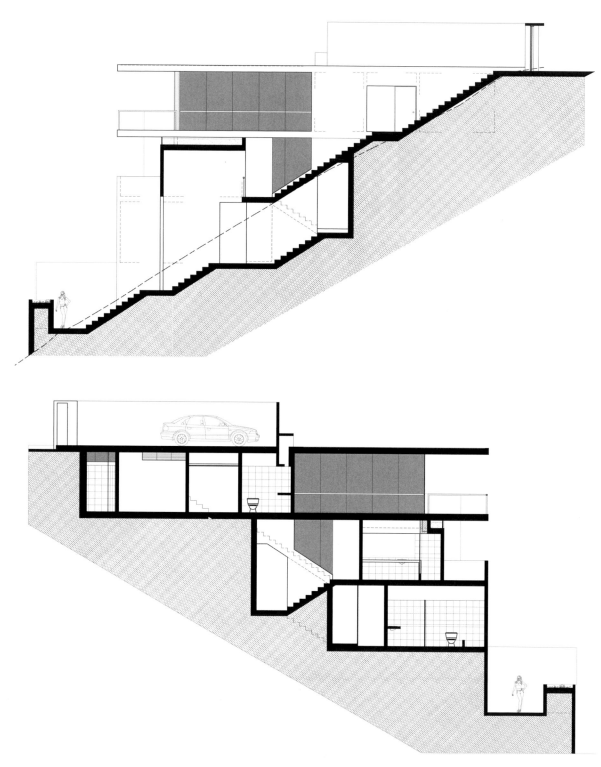

Sections

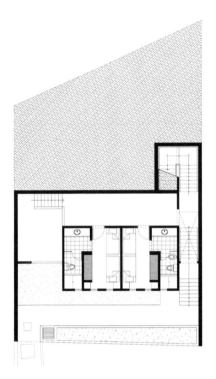

Third level plan

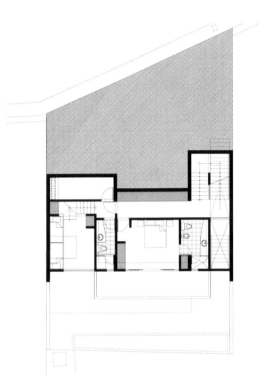

Second level plan

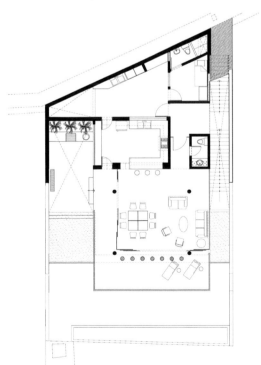

First level plan

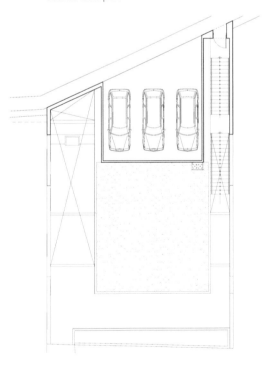

Entrance level plan

The water feature is designed to convey a sense of weightlessness, so the house literally feels as though it is floating.

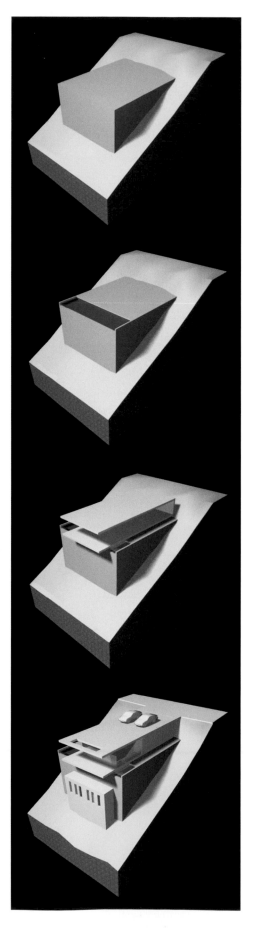

Evolution schemes

RESIDENCE IN ANCIENT CORINTH

Corinth, Greece   2008

This residence is located on the site of Ancient Corinth, Greece. This area is an archaeological site, where an excavation was previously made and which the project aimed to conserve. The relation between the building and its special landscape was also to be maintained, while care would be given to the site's historical legacy. These parameters resulted in a design program that was both functional and symbolic.

The house has a square shell—a block that serves to enclose the structure and demarcate the excavation area. It also serves as a reminder of its existence. Inside this shell, the residence was designed as an independent building rising vertically from the ground and seeking to spread itself over the ancient structures. Parallel to this, the southern section of the excavation is open to view, serving as evidence of continuity and conservation in the space covered by the building.

The structure of the house is metal with separate concrete frames covered in a double layer of cement. This system combines minimum air loss with excellent acoustic properties provided by the rigid structure. The use of white and double walls reduces solar incidence, offering considerable refrigeration loads during the summer months.

The home has two different levels: the layout of the different spaces is appreciated on the lower level, which is permanently in contact with both interior and exterior spaces. The upper level, however, is set apart by a design that is both open and closed; contact with the exterior through views are limited to perforations in the outer shell.

ARCHITECT
Spiros Papadopoulos

COLLABORATORS
E. Mantzari, N. Gousiaki, G. Iliadis, S. Papadatos (project team); Aris Tsagrasoulis/Building physics (consultant); Spiti S.A., Monotherm S.A. (general contractor)

TOTAL SURFACE AREA
2,260 sq ft

PHOTOGRAPHY
© Charalampos Louizidis

Perforations in the block-like shell allow the upper level to be open to and closed from the panoramic views. The use of white and double walls reduces solar incidence, cooling the house during the summer months.

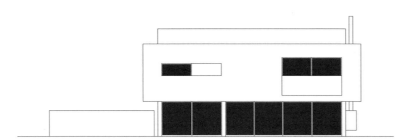

North elevation

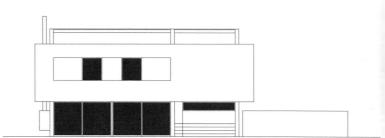

South elevation

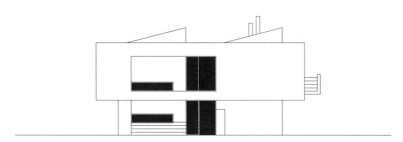

East elevation

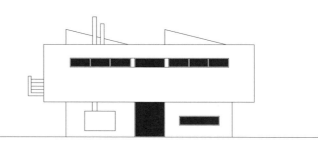

West elevation

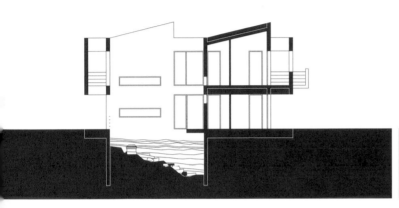

Section 1-1

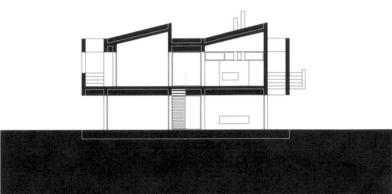

Section 2-2

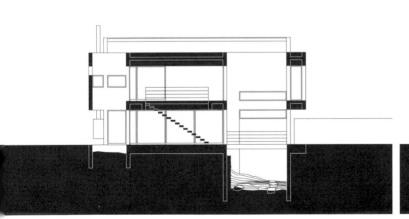

Section 3-3

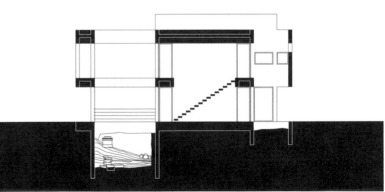

Section 4-4

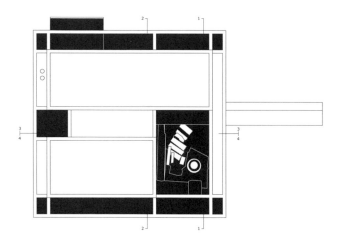

Roof plan

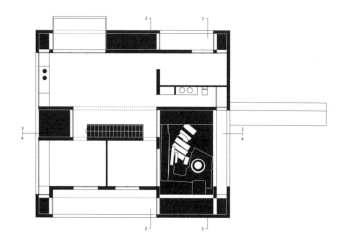

First floor plan

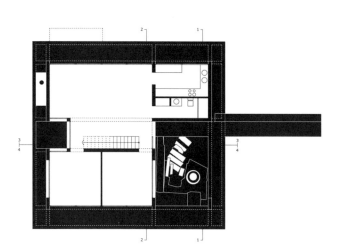

Ground floor plan

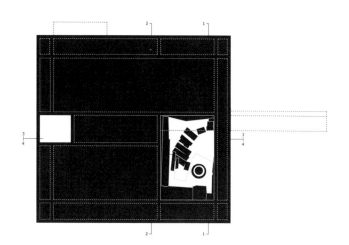

Excavation plan

VILLA P

Selb, Germany   2008

Designed by a team of three architects and winner of the Jury's Award for "good building" at the International Code Council 2008, this project involved the partial rebuilding and restoration of a previously standing residence in Selb, a town in the Wunsiedel district of the Bavarian region of Upper Franconia in Germany.

Conceptually, this home is a readaptation to the lifestyle of the new occupants, not their traditional middle-class grandparents who lived in the house. It was meant to house the following generations and respond to their modern-day needs and desires. The spaces needed to be recycled to make the home more dynamic and to enable transit through the various spaces to be freer and easier.

The home was originally built in 1956. As the property was enlarged, the residence was laid out on one level. The design was able to connect internal spaces with the landscape and create a visual link with it. The rebuilding, recycling, and restoration program paid special attention to the area called Patios. This is an exterior space at the heart of the home, that both separates and connects the interior with the exterior in a functional exchange.

There is also a south and west orientation with a terrace, part of a passive-energy-strategy design. This combination also included the existing living area, which guaranteed new qualities of use for the courtyard. The rebuild guaranteed a home custom-made to fit the needs of its occupants, a new framework for the old building, and a series of magnificent views.

ARCHITECT
Antje Osterwold, Matthias Schmidt/
Osterwold + Schmidt Architekten

COLLABORATORS
Plandrei Architekten
(landscape architect)

TOTAL SURFACE AREA
6,469 sq ft

PHOTOGRAPHY
© Steffen Groß, Michael Miltzow

Rebuilding the house, which was originally erected in 1956, focused on connecting the rooms visually with the landscape around it. Special attention was paid to the courtyard, which was conceived and designed as another space inside the property, despite the fact that it was outdoors.

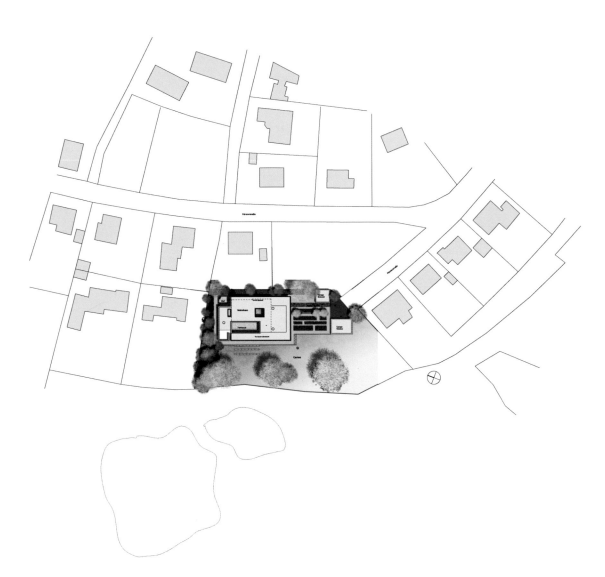

Site plan

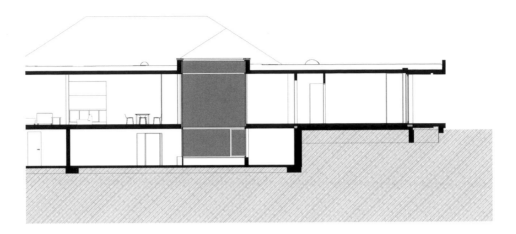

Section A-A

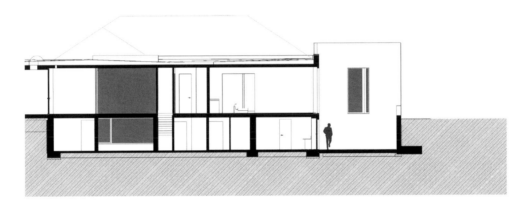

Section B-B

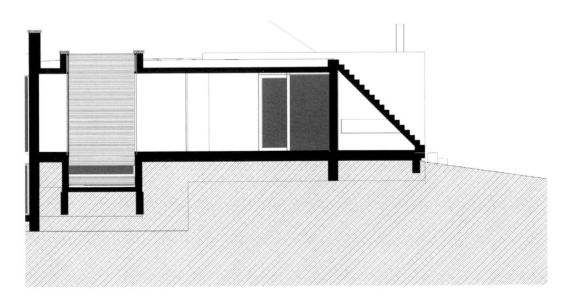

Section C-C

AATRIAL HOUSE

Opole, Poland   2006

This house is located in the vicinity of Opole, a city in the south of Poland on the Oder River. The site is in a residential development of typically 1970s-style cube houses not far from a forest.

The project had considered lowering the driveway to below ground level in order to separate it from the garden. This led to another idea: a driveway that passed under the building. An inner atrium was created for this purpose, where the driveway ends in a parking area.

The resulting building is open on all sides, with its terraces in an unrestricted manner. The only way of accessing the garden is through the atrium and the house. This made a new model of home possible, the opposite of an atrial house. This aatrial house is, instead, closed to the interior and open to its surroundings. The entrance is located at the highest point of the site on an east-facing slope. Following the gradient of the slope, the 33 ft (10 m) wide driveway passes under the lower level of the house, while the garden is partially raised over this level. As a result, the garden is separated from the driveway and the surrounding area by a 8 ft (2.5 m) high wall.

The design stretches and bends the surfaces of the cube. This principle creates the structure of the house and defines the interior and exterior architecture, including the use of materials. The house is a concrete monolith with finishes in the same material. Additional features are in ebony. The driveway and its walls are in quarried blocks of granite, a material typical of the surrounding area.

ARCHITECT
Robert Konieczny/KWK PROMES

COLLABORATORS
Marlena Wolnik, Lukasz Prazuch
(design team)

TOTAL SURFACE AREA
7,102 sq ft

PHOTOGRAPHY
© KWK PROMES

This building is located on the same level as the garden. In keeping with the style of houses in the area, the structure is the result of transformations made to a cube: the design stretches and bends its surfaces.

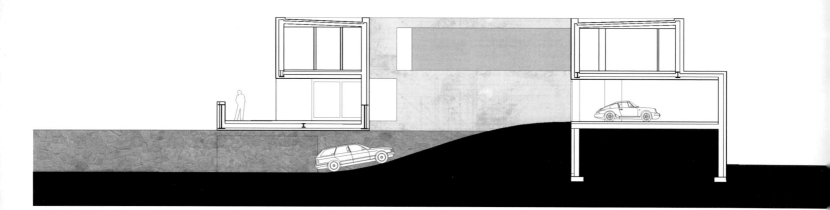

Section

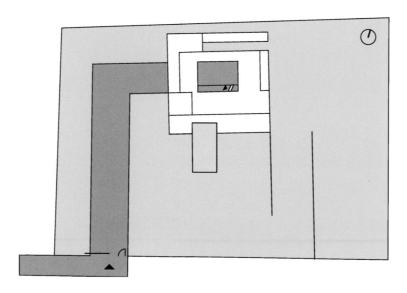

Site plan

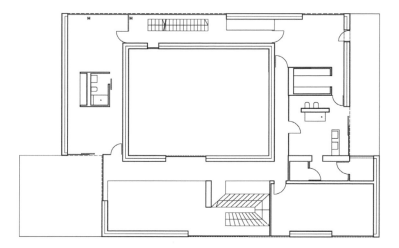

Ground floor plan

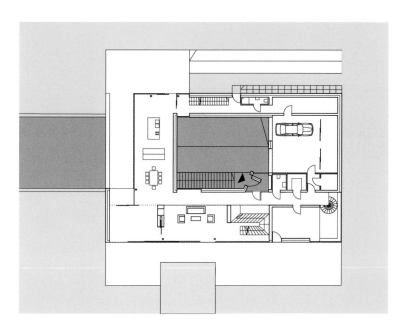

First floor plan

HOUSE IN LA ENCANTADA

Lima, Peru   2010

La Encantada is a single-family home named for the coastal suburb of Lima where it is located. This home was laid out as a series of planes intersected by a creased plane. The home is noteworthy in its fluid design sensibility. The interior design speaks to the exterior garden design, and the resulting architectural dialogue informs the highly livable yet aesthetically pleasing home. The upper level of the two-story container holds the private areas—the main bedroom and three children's bedrooms. This level is connected to a terrace that affords garden views. The lower level contains the public spaces, including the living/dining areas, kitchen, home office, and service areas. The two levels are connected by a staircase located in an area with a double-height void. This staircase can be seen from the entrance to the home.

ARCHITECT
Javier Artadi/Artadi Arquitectos

TOTAL SURFACE AREA
3,115.6 sq ft

PHOTOGRAPHY
© Elsa Ramírez

There is ample transit space in this home as well as a fluid architectural sensibility. This fluidity is perhaps best exemplified by the upper level's terraces, which extend the interior space to the exterior.

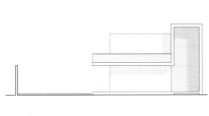

East façade

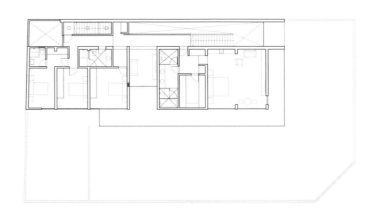

First floor plan

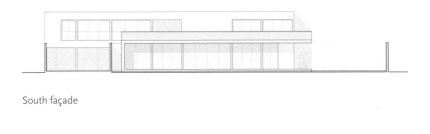

South façade

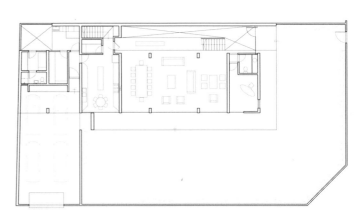

Ground floor plan

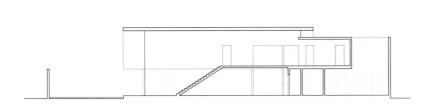

Longitudinal section

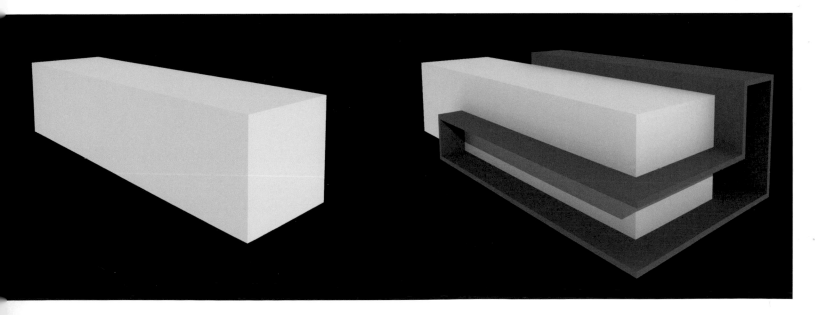

olution schemes

STAR HOUSE

Bnaider, Kuwait 2009

The Star House is located on the Kuwait coast. Initially designed as three free-standing houses facing the sea, the design was changed to accommodate a large central house, two small guest bungalows, and a boat house. The residence is incredibly private. The site was intentionally chosen for its remote location; there are no other buildings nearby. The buildings' stone façade protects the residence from contact with the desert and possible erosion.

ARCHITECT
Nasser Abulhasan, Joaquín Pérez Goicoechea/AGi Architects

COLLABORATORS
Georg Thesing, Abdul Hafiz Mohammed, Robert A. Varghese, Bruno Afonso Martins Gomes, Moyra Montoya Moyano (project team); MIMAR, Estructuras Arturo Macusi (consultant)

TOTAL SURFACE AREA
53,820 sq ft

COST
$6,993,251.52

PHOTOGRAPHY
© Nelson Garrido

Huge windows beautifully frame
expansive views of the sea.

Level +15.00

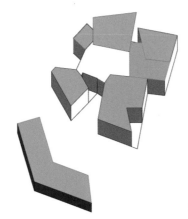

Access level +11.00

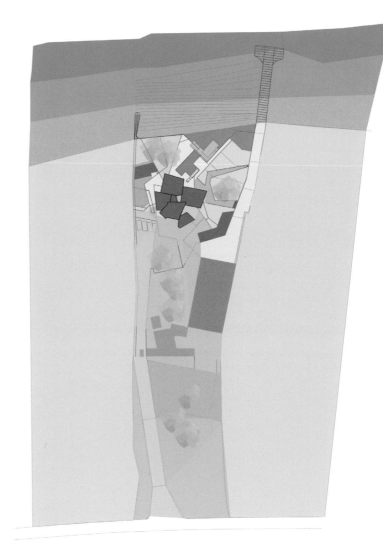

Site plan

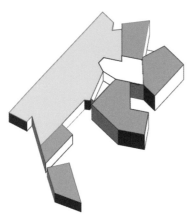

Level +6.00

Key area schemes

■ Living area
■ Private area
□ Staff area

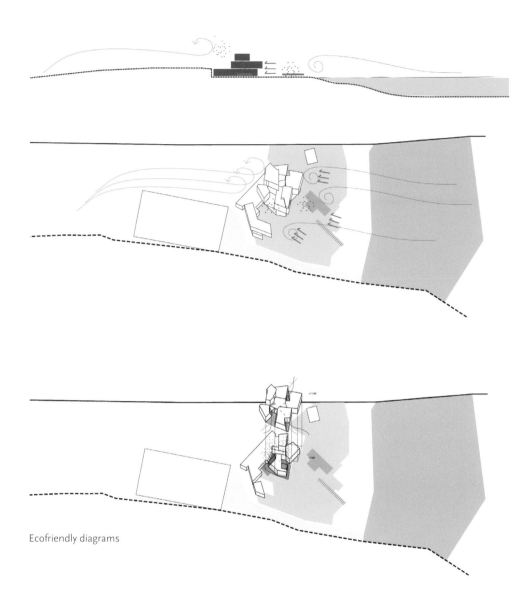

Ecofriendly diagrams

First floor plan

Ground floor plan

The home has numerous and varied spaces. Among them is this public area where the predominant feature is white. The small inner garden serves as an area for relaxation and brings nature into the interior of the home.

DEVOTO HOUSE

Buenos Aires, Argentina   2009

This residence is located in Villa Devoto, a Buenos Aires suburb. Two challenges the team faced when designing the house were the poor views and the fact that there is little exposure to daylight, the result of being hidden in the shadows of neighboring buildings. To overcome these obstacles, the team focused on creating an internal landscape that would produce better views.

As the dwelling was very large relative to the total surface area of the site, the architects decided to leave the first floor area as austere as possible. As a result, they managed to open a large amount of space for a larger leisure area. Unlike more conventional homes, where the garden is at the rear, the outdoor space was purposefully located at the entrance. This design decision inverted the layout, so that the kitchen and the living room moved to the back of the lot. The home is laid out as a series of steps. The bedrooms are located on the lower floor facing east over the heart of the home—the garden. The upper level houses a relaxation area especially designed for the older family members. It contains a spa bath, a sauna, a fitness room, and a large terrace with views over the garden.

ARCHITECT
Andrés Remy Arquitectos

COLLABORATORS
Andrés Remy, Hernán Pardillos, Julieta Rafel, Carlos Arellano, Lilian Kandus (design team)

TOTAL SURFACE AREA
5,920 sq ft

PHOTOGRAPHY
© Alejandro Peral

In order to find the best location for the swimming pool, the team conducted a site analysis and reviewed data from a solar incidence sensor.

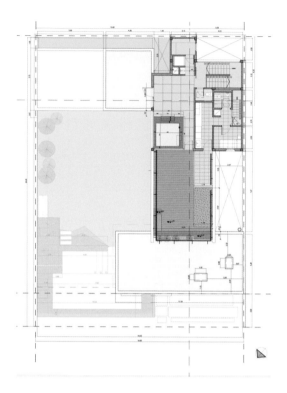

Second floor plan

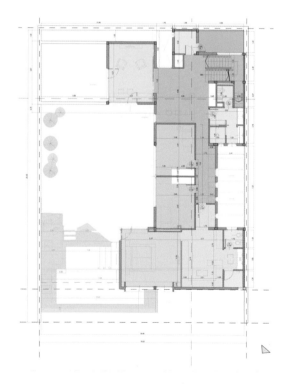

First floor plan

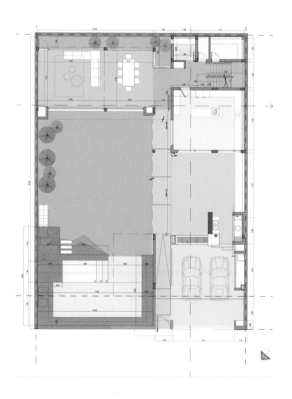

Ground floor plan

NEGRA HOUSE

Benavídez, Argentina   2007

This single-family home is positioned right in the middle of a suburb of Buenos Aires, about 18 miles (30 km) from downtown. Site analysis proved that the most impressive views over the surrounding lake were to be had from the rear. However, the best orientation was from the street front, where the site narrowed.

The house was designed for a socially active couple without children, which made the program relatively simple. Greatest importance was given to the social aspect. The public area is divided into two parts. One part satisfies everyday use, and houses the kitchen and dining area. The other, located at the front of the house, contains the living area with lake views. The living area has no partitions and a number of its walls are totally glazed. It is also on a different level from the rest of the floor, which provides visual permeability with the other areas. Both programs are connected by glass bridge that spans water that seems to disappear while it flows under the feet of those crossing it.

The upper floor continues the same program of spatial division. The future children's bedrooms were positioned at the front of the house with two large floor-to-ceiling windows overlooking the lake. The master bedroom suite, like a bridge spanning the space between the two volumes, is located on the lower level. This cantilevered space features the best views and seems to float over the lake.

ARCHITECT
Andrés Remy Arquitectos

COLLABORATORS
Andrés Remy, Hernán Pardillos, Julieta Rafel, Carlos Arellano, Gisela Colombo (design team)

TOTAL SURFACE AREA
3,552 sq ft

PHOTOGRAPHY
© Alejandro Peral, Gustavo Sosa Pinilla

The austerity of this home is almost provocative. The immaculate white open-plan exterior contrasts with the totally black exterior. This contrast is so distinguished that the house was christened La Casa Negra ("the black house").

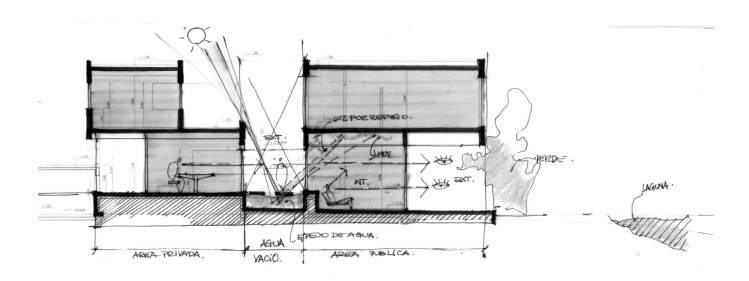

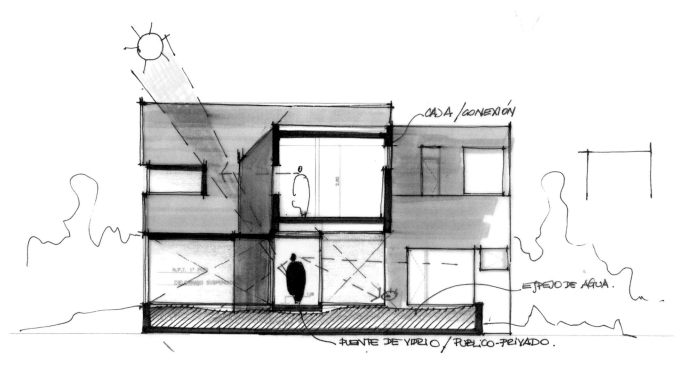

Section sketches

The floor-to-ceiling windows offer
dramatic views of the lake.

Ground floor plan

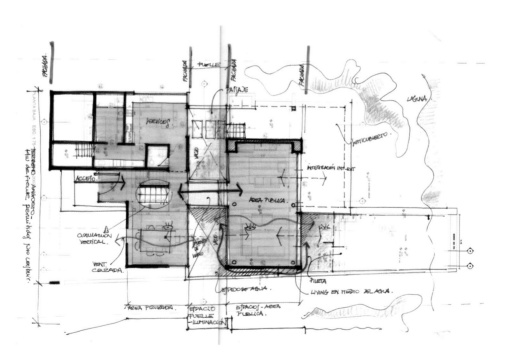

Plan sketch

RZ HOUSE

Benavídez, Argentina   2006

Built on a 2,906 sq ft (270 m²) site in Benavídez, the northern part of the Buenos Aires metropolitan area, this single-family home features two interlocking volumes. The entrance is located where the two volumes intersect. Due to various site and terrain characteristics, the home has a J-shaped floor plan, which affords the best views without lessening the privacy of the nonpublic areas. The rear façade windows frame the different views of the surrounding landscape while the street frontage has eye-level horizontal openings that showcase the nearby lake. The house's most interesting feature is its relation to the swimming pool, which was not only designed with a recreational purpose, but also to aid in maintaining a comfortable temperature in the house; the pool water captures and reflects light, thereby creating a microclimate for the areas that surround it.

ARCHITECT
Andrés Remy Arquitectos

COLLABORATORS
Andrés Remy, Amy Brown, Flavia Bellani, Paula Mancini, Sofía Focaccia (design team)

TOTAL SURFACE AREA
2,906 sq ft

PHOTOGRAPHY
© Alejandro Peral

The swimming pool helps regulate the
residence's temperature, making it
both functional and recreational.

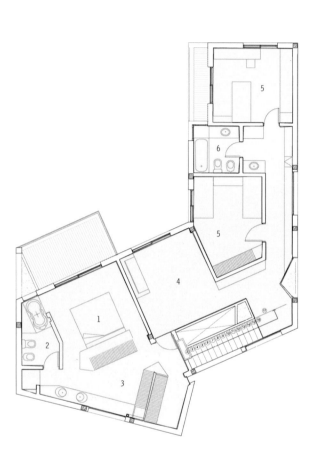

First floor plan

1. Main bedroom
2. Main bathroom
3. Wardrobe
4. Playroom
5. Bedroom
6. Bathroom

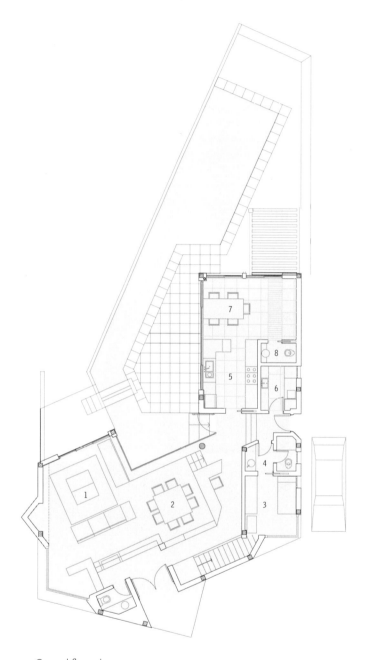

Ground floor plan

1. Living room
2. Dining room
3. Service room
4. Service bathroom
5. Kitchen
6. Laundry room
7. Breakfast room
8. Bathroom

RM HOUSE

Laguna del Sol, Argentina   2005

Located in Laguna del Sol, a suburb 25 minutes outside of downtown Buenos Aires, this single-family home is specifically designed for an active family—a young couple and their two children—who spend a lot of their time at home entertaining. The project was designed around the family's needs. The house was divided into two levels connected by an intermediate space that serves as a playroom. The lower level houses the public areas, and features split levels with different flooring materials; the polished cement floors are for the recreation spaces, and the cherrywood floors are for the transit areas. The lower level also contains an indoor "green" area. A virtual lung for the house, this garden space has extra-tall windows to welcome in the light.

An important vertical connection leads to the intermediate area, where the home theater system is located, and to the upper level, where the private spaces are housed. The master bedroom is separated from the children's bedrooms by green spaces. The garden is a lush oasis of greenery, featuring a pool with hydromassage system. The pool deck is integrated into the garden.

The project was for a site measuring 8,200 sq ft (760 m²). Of this, only 3,230 sq ft (300 m²) were set aside for the house. The rest was reserved for the all-encompassing garden. Certainly the modern-looking architecture sets it apart from neighboring homes. The garden is another stand-out feature.

ARCHITECT
Andrés Remy Arquitectos

COLLABORATORS
Andrés Remy, Flavia Bellani, Marcos Pozzo, Paula Mancini, Laura Rodríguez Segat, Leandra Rodríguez Llebana (design team)

TOTAL SURFACE AREA
3,230 sq ft

PHOTOGRAPHY
© Alejandro Peral

Modern architecture is softened by the lush garden and the swimming pool. As luxurious as it is stunning, this home stands apart from the neighboring buildings.

First floor plan

1. Main bedroom
2. Wardrobe
3. Main bathroom
4. Playroom
5. Bedroom
6. Bathroom
7. Storage room
8. Terrace

Ground floor plan

1. Living room
2. Dining room
3. Kitchen
4. Grill
5. Laundry room
6. Service room
7. Service bathroom
8. Toilet
9. Office

Section and elevations

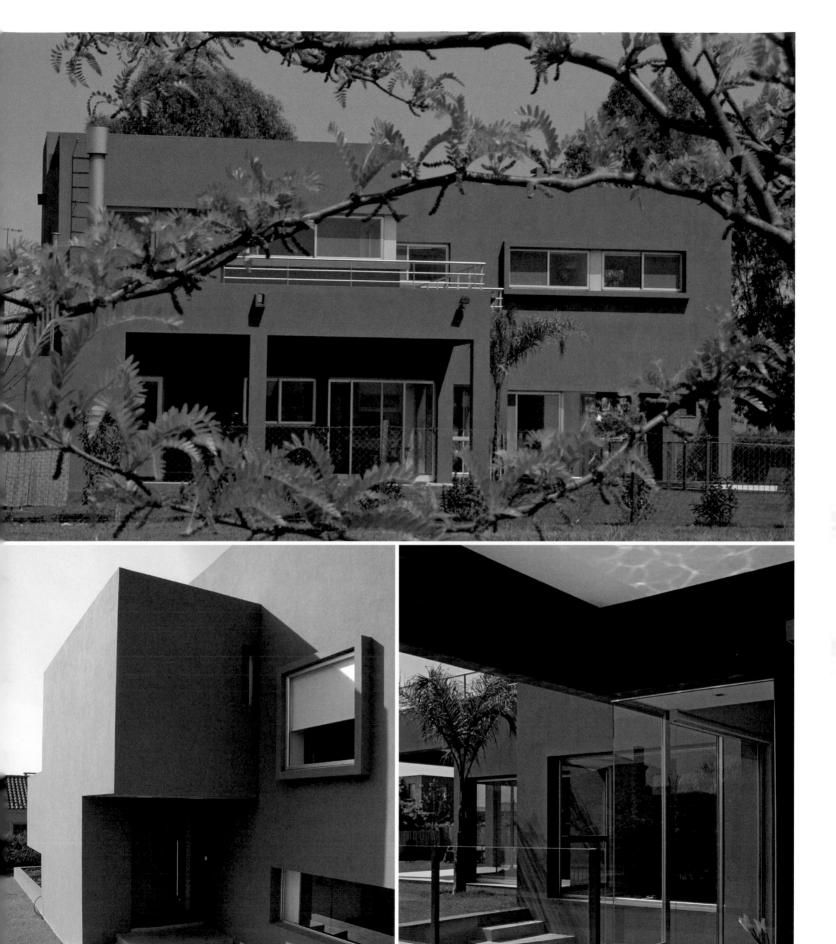

GOLD COAST BEACH HOUSE

Gold Coast, QLD, Australia   2008

This beach house is located on Australia's Gold Coast. This home was designed to replace a house the client already had standing on the site.

The basic idea of the design program was to turn one of the two undercover levels into an open-air space. It was hoped that this would connect the residence with the garden, from which there were spectacular views over the Broadwater.

The compact construction maintains the typical features of the area's urban fabric. The house stands 5 ft (1.5 m) above street level. This height enables the views of the beach from the garden to be enhanced. This design also fulfills other functions like giving the occupants privacy and improving the public use of streets. This home also has a large number of windows along its length that ensure good natural ventilation. The placement of floor-to-ceiling windows on the northeast and west façades reduces the entry of sunlight in summer while allowing abundant daylight into the house in winter.

The materials used include concrete on most of the external walls. Some stretches of wall have a wood frame lined with fiber cement panels. The roof is steel framed and the floor is in white terrazzo, although some areas are floored in natural wood.

Other features of the house are the guestroom, bathroom, utility room, and first floor garden. The upper level contains the master bedroom, living area, office, and second bedroom. The basement level is for parking and storage.

ARCHITECT
Steve McCracken, Darren Greenaway/
BDA Architecture

TOTAL SURFACE AREA
592 sq ft

PHOTOGRAPHY
© Scott Burrows/Aperture Architectural
Photography

The opening in the structure connecting the home
with the garden offers residents one of the best
views of the beach. This connection provides a fluid
dialogue between open and closed areas of the home.

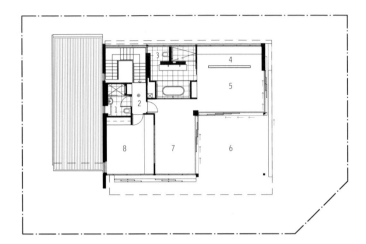

First floor plan

1. Bathroom 2
2. Hall
3. En suite bathroom
4. Dressing room
5. Master bedroom
6. Void
7. Living room
8. Studio

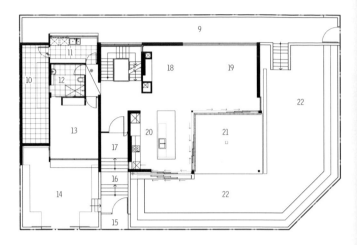

Ground floor plan

9. Service yard
10. Drying court
11. Laundry room
12. Bathroom 1
13. Guest room
14. Driveway
15. Entry
16. Landing
17. Entry
18. Dining room
19. Living room
20. Kitchen
21. Lanai
22. Garden

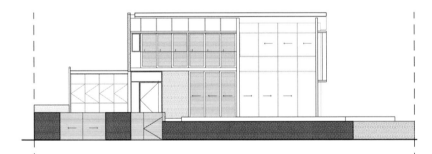

North elevation

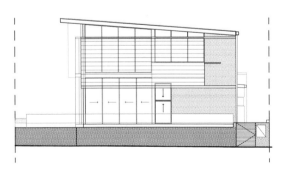

West elevation

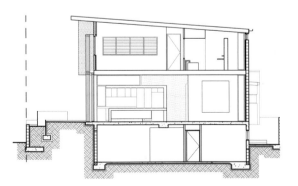

Typical elevation

BUNDY RESIDENCE

Brentwood, CA, USA   2008

This home, located in a neighborhood populated with ranch-style houses, underwent a full remodeling that involved the redesign of some of its spaces. The kitchen, for example, was moved to a larger space that enabled new countertops, furniture, and central islands to be installed, which provided more working areas. The lighting system was also redesigned.

The new design strengthened the relationships between the different spaces, resulting, for example, in a better transit flow between the kitchen and the rear patio. The existing relationship between the kitchen ceiling and the attic was modified to provide more daylight and greater volume to the former.

The idea of increased volume and more fluid connections between interior and exterior spaces led to the living room being positioned between the two. Articulated forms are a feature of the ceiling, which continues through the exposed roof beams. Glass doors open to the patio and provide a fluid connection between interior and exterior.

ARCHITECT
Eric Rosen Architects

COLLABORATORS
Eric Rosen (principal); Lesley Graham (project manager); Carlos Valenzuela, Braden LeMaster (project team); Martin Gantman/Martin Gantman Studio (structural engineer); Rotondi Construction (general contractor)

TOTAL SURFACE AREA
2,500 sq ft

PHOTOGRAPHY
© Erich Koyama

The interior features high white ceilings.
The design boldly mixes materials, such
as wood, plaster, and metal.

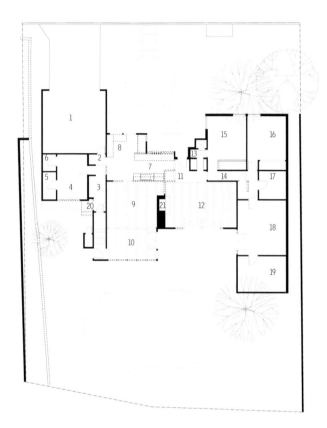

Pre-existing plan

1. Garage
2. Garage entry
3. Laundry room
4. Maid's quarters
5. Maid's bathroom
6. Maid's closet
7. Kitchen
8. Breakfast area
9. Family room
10. Dining room
11. Entry
12. Living room
13. Powder room
14. Hall
15. Bedroom 1
16. Bedroom 2
17. Bathroom
18. Master bedroom
19. Master bathroom
20. Back entry
21. Fireplace

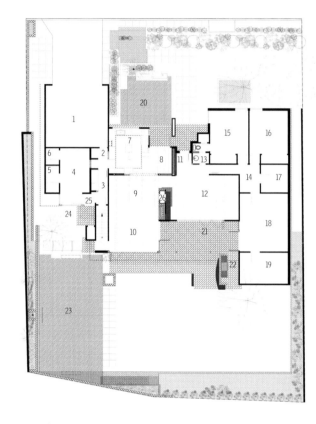

New plan

1. Garage
2. Garage entry
3. Laundry room
4. Maid's quarters
5. Maid's bathroom
6. Maid's closet
7. Kitchen
8. Breakfast area
9. Family room
10. Dining room
11. Entry
12. Living room
13. Powder room
14. Hall
15. Bedroom 1
16. Bedroom 2
17. Bathroom
18. Master bedroom
19. Master bathroom
20. Front patio
21. Covered patio
22. Barbecue
23. Sport court
24. Garden
25. Back entry
26. Fireplace

SAFE HOUSE

Warsaw, Poland 2009

The aptly named Safe House is located in a small village on the outskirts of Warsaw. The brief was to create a feeling of maximum security. It is cube-shaped with movable exterior parts. The innovative part of this project consists of the use of moving walls. When the house is closed at night, the security zone is limited to the outline of the house. When its walls are opened during the daytime, this zone extends to the garden.

The Safe House project offers a new type of building where operation is more important than form. It was built incorporating technically complex design solutions. The sliding walls, both 7.25 ft (2.2 m) tall and 49 ft (15 m) and 72 ft (22 m) long, allow the urban structure to be interfered with and define the security zone. All the movable features work with electric motors, which help to guarantee safe operation. The building is a concrete monolith, while the movable parts are made of light steel frames with mineral wool infill. The result is a building that is excellently insulated.

The façade is finished in plywood and cement fixed to a dark steel structure. It is meant to resemble the wood features of the surrounding houses, enabling it to blend in with the surrounding rural landscape. The interior is a light-filled space that blends extensively with the garden. Glazed expanses behind the movable walls allow the building to acquire energy on winter days and prevent the summer sun from overheating the house.

ARCHITECT
Robert Konieczny/KWK PROMES

COLLABORATORS
Marcin Jojko, Lukasz Zadrzynski (design team); Magdalena Radalowicz-Zadrzynska (interior designer)

TOTAL SURFACE AREA
6,098 sq ft

PHOTOGRAPHY
© KWK PROMES

The thick outer layer enables the house to store energy for when it is closed at night. It has a hybrid heating and ventilation system that makes the house an intelligent passive building.

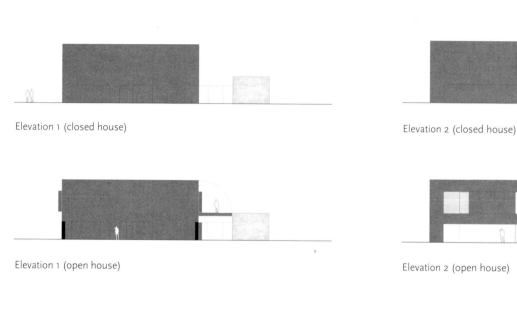

Elevation 1 (closed house)

Elevation 2 (closed house)

Elevation 1 (open house)

Elevation 2 (open house)

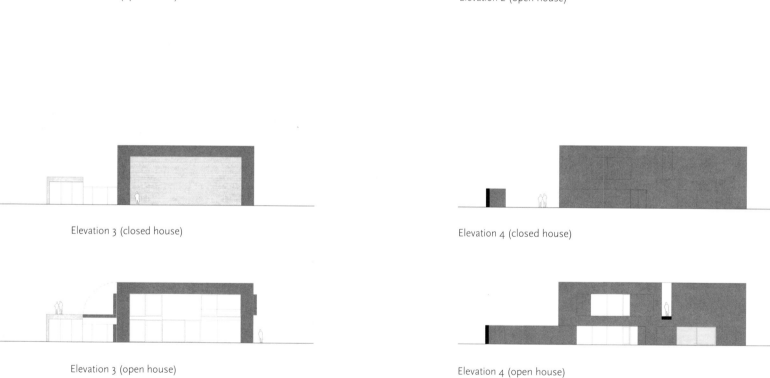

Elevation 3 (closed house)

Elevation 4 (closed house)

Elevation 3 (open house)

Elevation 4 (open house)

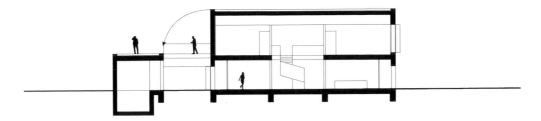

Cross section

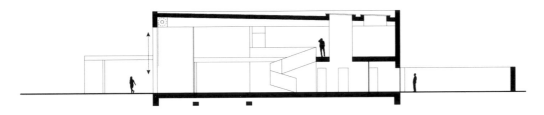

Longitudinal section

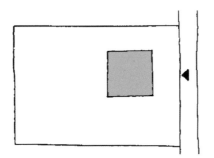

Safe zone when the house is closed (sketch)

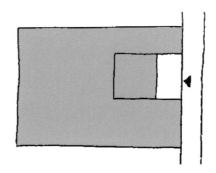

Safe zone when the house is open (sketch)

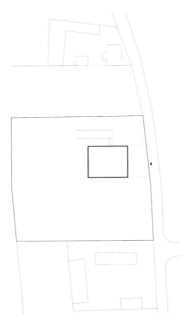

Site plan

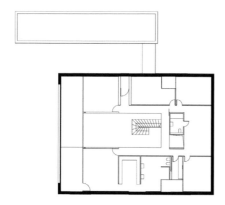

First floor (closed house)

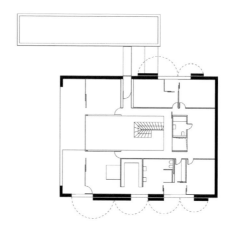

First floor (open house)

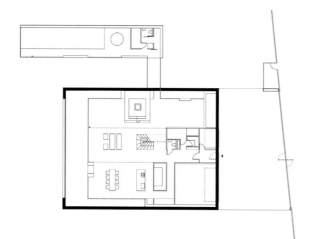

Ground floor (closed house)

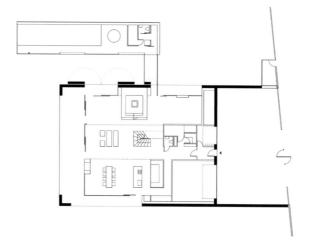

Ground floor (open house)

EHRLICH RESIDENCE

Santa Monica, CA, USA   2004

The team had three specific goals when creating this house: continuous space, access to natural light, and a strong relationship between indoors and outdoors. The architects hoped to create a sustainable south-facing house with ample light and circulated air, covering as much as surface as possible, and surrounded by gardens. The lower level is L-shaped, with the spaces revolving around the garage and the garden. Large eaves block the summer sun on the south side while allowing the winter sun to warm the concrete floor, which serves as a heating source.

The house is clad in two self-sustaining materials: drywall panels and concrete. The garage door is lined in stainless steel. The wood on the main door, the internal staircases, and the upper level was special-

ly harvested. There is a 4 kW photovoltaic system on the roof.

Concealed within this relatively orthogonal design is a series of diagonal openings. These openings let the natural breeze in to circulate between the office and the vestibule, then into the dining area, and finally into the kitchen, which is located on the north side to take advantage of the morning light.

The vertical lines of the atrium contrast with the horizontal lines of the lower level. A mixture of reflected and direct light illuminates the interior during the day, and creates a soft sheen at night. The upstairs bedrooms, particularly the master bedroom, with its internal window, are organized around this space. This room makes the most of its three-way orientation, giving it a treehouse-like feeling.

ARCHITECT
John Friedman Alice Kimm Architects

COLLABORATORS
John Friedman (principal-in-charge); Alice Kimm, Leigh Christy, John Martin, Pauline Shu (project team); Anthony Bonomo/Bonomo Development (general contractor)

TOTAL SURFACE AREA
3,500 sq ft

PHOTOGRAPHY
© Benny Chan/Fotoworks

The lower level is L-shaped, with the spaces
revolving around the garage and the garden.
Large eaves block the summer sun on the south
side while allowing the winter sun to warm the
concrete floor, which serves as a heating source.

HOUSE IN LAKE OKOBOJI

West Lake Okoboji, IA, USA   2008

Two and a half hours away from the nearest metropolitan area, this home is located on the shores of Lake Okoboji in Iowa, in a neighborhood where old cottages sit together with new mansions. The strategy pursued by the architects was to reduce the perimeter of the house on the ground to a minimum while at the same time creating huge windows that would enable the occupants to enjoy the views outside but prevent the neighbors from looking in.

The design is a simple volume with an opaque wood-slat façade cladding spatial tubes. The exterior structure opens to lake and forest views. View-framing windows that resemble tubes are literally voids in the mass of the house, bounded only by glass. Light and air enter the rooms through these windows. The first level of the house is dominated by a subtle and amorphous space that marks the layout of the main living areas while suggesting connections and extensions to the surrounding lake and sky.

ARCHITECT
Min | Day

CLIENT
Paul and Annette Smith

COLLABORATORS
E.B. Min, Jeffrey L. Day (partners-in-charge); Nicholas Papefthimiou, Kristine Mummert, Matt Cavin, Christina Kaneva, Jeff Davis, Matt Goldsberry, Christina Richards, Natalie Kittner (project team); Mike Hoien Construction (general contractor); Aaron Carlson (millwork)

TOTAL SURFACE AREA
6,000 sq ft

PHOTOGRAPHY
© Larry Gawel, John Reed Forsman, Paul Crosby

The colors that appear in the drawings of the ground floor, second floor, and third floor allude to the different modular tubes used in the construction of the house. Piled up, these tubes allow a physical and visual connection with the outside.

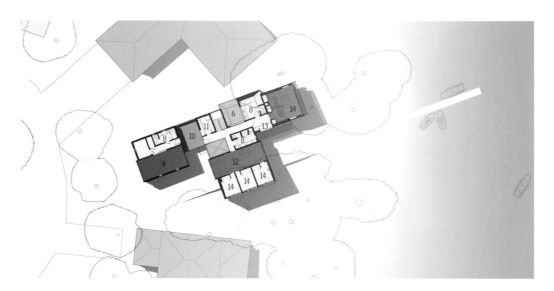

Second floor plan

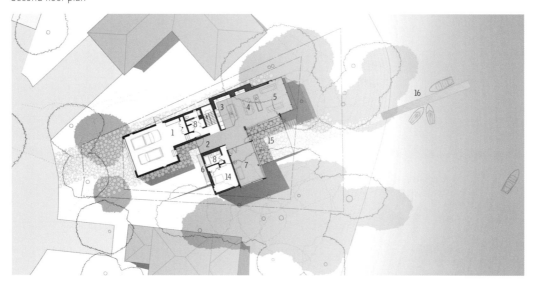

First floor plan

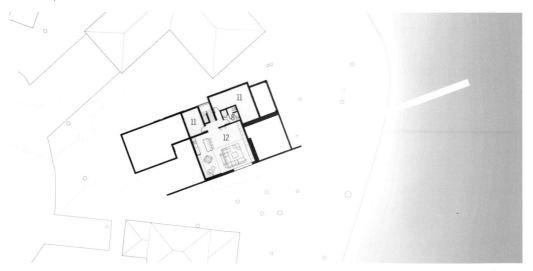

Basement plan

1. Garage/storage room
2. Entry
3. Kitchen
4. Dining room
5. Living room
6. Skylight
7. Screened porch
8. Bathroom
9. Bunk room
10. Wood terrace
11. Utility room
12. Playroom
13. Studio
14. Bedroom
15. Terrace
16. Dock

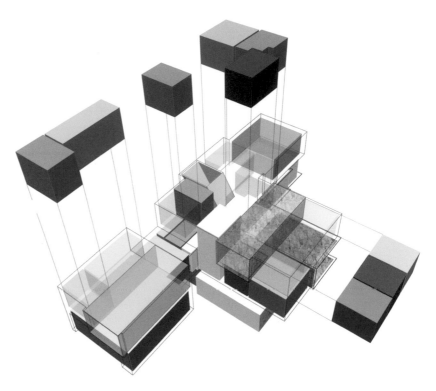

Exploded axonometric

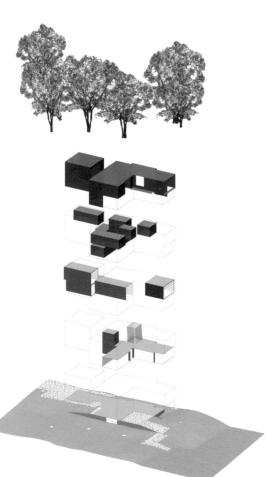

Exploded axonometric

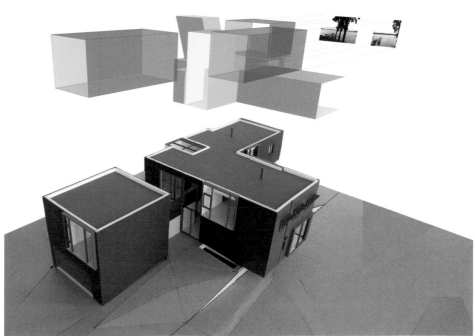

Diagrams

STEINHARDT PITTMAN RESIDENCE

Birmingham, MI, USA   2008

Located in an urban area, this home was built for a typical family. Its program included the use of natural, modern, recycled, and technologically advanced materials, such as cement fiber panels that form a barrier to the elements. The garage, while being located underground, welcomes in daylight through wide openings along the length of the façade. Large skylights also enable light to penetrate through this hermetic design. The house is laid out over three floors, occupying 2,665 sq ft (247 m²) of space that consists of a foyer, living area, dining area, porch, kitchen, family room, dressing room, master bedroom suite, two service rooms, three bathrooms, storeroom, utility room, and fitness room.

Light enters the first floor through large floor-to-ceiling windows at both ends of the house. The light is controlled by Solarfective sunshades, which also give residents a sense of privacy.

No partitions separate, define, or organize the space of the living area; this task is left to the furniture, which consist of a large sofa and leather and chrome armchairs set against a backdrop of an old Persian carpet. The black granite fireplace is the heart of this room. Abundant daylight entering the first floor rises to the master bedroom through floor-to-ceiling windows, and a metal staircase leads to the second floor.

ARCHITECT
McIntosh Poris Associates

CLIENT
Janice Steinhardt, Mark Pittman

COLLABORATORS
Michael Poris (principal-in-charge);
Alex Rockwell, Aaron Taylor, Liron Cohen
(design); Janice Steinhardt,
MDG Design (interior designer)

TOTAL SURFACE AREA
2,665 sq ft

PHOTOGRAPHY
© Balthazar Korab

The roof design features a sharp angle. The façade is made from large rectangular fiber cement panels with window joinery in aluminum.

HOUSE IN COMANO

Comano, Switzerland   2007

This house is located in Comano, a small village in the Swiss canton of Ticino, north of Lugano, located in the foothills of the Alps. Laid out on a hillside, it appears as a kind of boundary between the mountains and the recently developed flatter areas. The steeply sloping site suggests that the terrain is an architectural feature, as if a part of the built volume of the house.

As the result of the vertical nature of the two stories, which are in compliance with strict local building codes, including height limits to preserve the view of the historic hilltop village, the building blends organically into the landscape. This layout gives the sensation of being in a bigger space, one that consists of different climate, material, and light conditions.

The house is made up of three concrete boxes and one glass box—the atrium.

Each box is raised half a height and topped with flat roofs. The interior spaces are connected to the exterior, and are made to appear to be a continuation of the interior, by means of clear and octagonal geometries featuring different materials: concrete, grass, and water.

The residence is laid out over different levels, intercalated from east to west over the site. The first level contains two bedrooms. The first interstitial mezzanine level holds two additional bedrooms and a bathroom. On the second level, a living area opens out to a large glassed space with views over the swimming pool. On the second mezzanine, the kitchen opens to the atrium with an inner garden. The large entrance porch, which is also a parking area, is dug into the hillside, leaving the upper volume as if "floating" in the garden.

ARCHITECT
Davide Macullo, Marco Strozzi/Davide Macullo Architects

CLIENT
Luana Tozzini Paglia, Raoul Paglia

COLLABORATORS
Laura Perolini, Margherita Pusterla, Michele Alberio (design team); Davide Macullo, Marco Strozzi (interior designer); Luigi Pellegrinelli/Ideal Ingegno SA (engineering); Franco Semini (physical engineering); Ennio Magetti (supervision)

TOTAL SURFACE AREA
2,153 sq ft

PHOTOGRAPHY
© Pino Musi, Enrico Cano

The ramp-like layout of the two floors connects each of the spaces, while the garden enhances the sensation of constantly being over the lower level of the house. A staircase connects the levels and offers the feeling of walking on the natural slope.

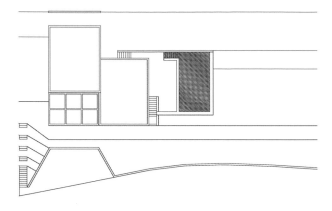

Roof level

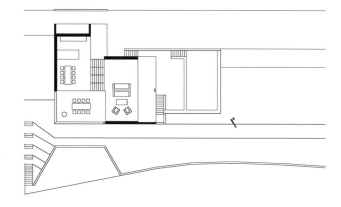

Level +6.03/+7.42

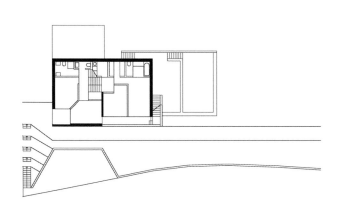

Level +3.25/+4.64

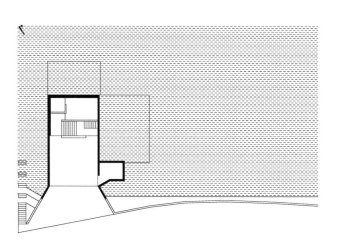

Level +0.30

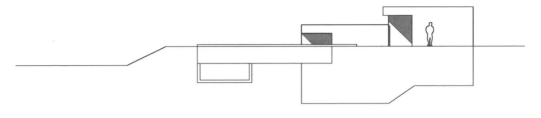

North elevation

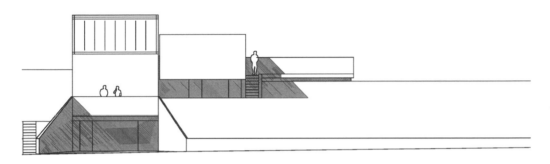

South elevation

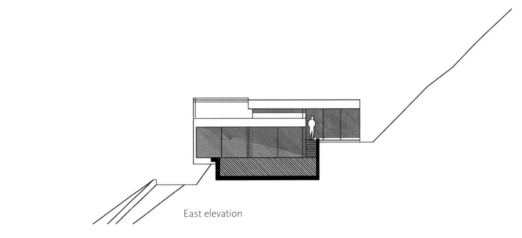

East elevation

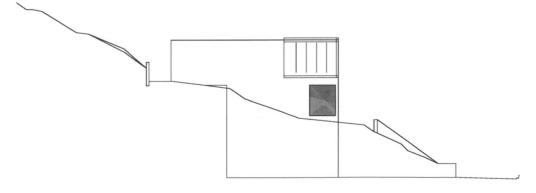

West elevation

HYBRID FORMS

MIAMI RESIDENCE

Miami Beach, QLD, Australia   2008

The urban features of the design of this daring beach house make the building stand out from its neighbors. The dwelling incorporates robust materials capable of withstanding the strong winds that tend to buffet the region. In order to resist these climatic conditions, the project was designed for building in layers using different types of strong materials such as perpender, a stone used to bind a structural wall with an interior cladding, such as wood and galvanized iron panels. Other methods were also used to battle adverse climatic conditions, such as steel frames and cantilevered beams, where one of the ends of the beam is embedded while the other hangs freely.

The home is located on a site measuring 33 ft (10 m) in length by 164 ft (50 m) in width. The fact that the lot was facing west created a large series of restrictions for the building program. The residence was designed to house a large family. In response to this requirement, it was laid out over three floors as public and private spaces needed by such a large group of people.

A central courtyard acts as a ventilation system. This occurs because many of the rooms feature floor-to-ceiling windows that open to the courtyard. This enables each of these rooms to benefit from cross ventilation, providing natural cooling.

ARCHITECT
Adam Beck, Erica Borgstrom/BDA Architecture

TOTAL SURFACE AREA
7,534.7 sq ft

PHOTOGRAPHY
© Scott Burrows/Aperture Architectural Photography

This home stands out because its urban look contrasts strongly with its beachside locations. Its construction makes use of robust materials capable of withstanding the strong winds that are typical of the area.

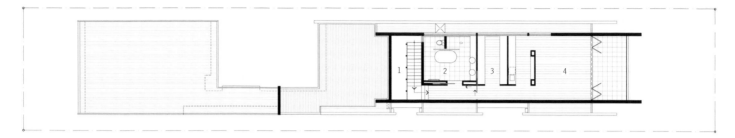

Second floor plan

1. Void
2. En suite bathroom 1
3. Walk-in wardrobe
4. Bedroom 1

First floor plan

5. Dressing room
6. En suite bathroom 2
7. Dressing room
8. Bedroom 3
9. Bedroom 4
10. Bedroom 2
11. En suite bathroom 3
12. Central courtyard
13. Gallery

14. Studio 1
15. Family room
16. Studio 2
17. Kitchen
18. Pantry
19. Powder room
20. Dining room
21. Living room
22. Deck

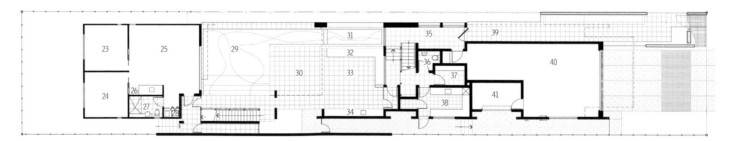

Ground floor plan

23. Bedroom 5
24. Bedroom 6
25. Multipurpose room
26. Bar
27. Bathroom
28. Laundry room 1
29. Pool
30. Central courtyard
31. Reflection pond
32. Sitting area

33. Lanai
34. Barbecue
35. Lobby
36. Toilet
37. Cellar
38. Laundry room 2
39. Entry
40. Garage
41. Storage room

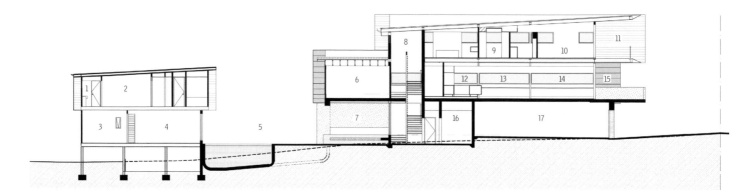

Typical section plan

1. En suite bathroom
2. Bedroom 4
3. Bedroom 6
4. Multipurpose room
5. Central courtyard
6. Family room
7. Lanai
8. Void
9. Walk-in wardrobe
10. Bedroom 1
11. Balcony
12. Kitchen
13. Dining room
14. Living room
15. Deck
16. Cellar
17. Garage

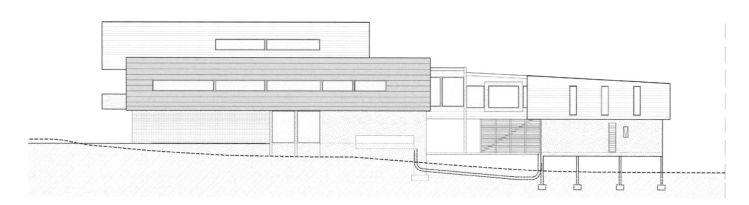

North elevation

East elevation

FACETED HOUSE 1

London, United Kingdom   2009

For this home in the neighborhood of Hammersmith, the architects remodelled and readapted a building that was in a state of ruin. The building design revolved around the idea of extending the existing space using a large open floor plan. A shift of 30° in the angle of the design gives the illusion of different spaces. The result is the experience of an overlapping view between covered and open-air spaces, such as that achieved with the kitchen and the garden ground surface. This concept is continued in some of the zinc façade details.

The owners wanted a practical space as well as one that was comfortable. To this end, the team designed a storage wall. This concealed closet was built at one end of the kitchen to hide the different elements used in this space. Electrical appliances were also concealed to create the simple space the client desired. The owners also wanted lots of natural light. The house contains lots of windows, sliding doors, special skylight panels in the roof, and pale, light-reflecting floors.

ARCHITECT
Paul McAneary, Mattias Laumayer/Paul McAneary Architects

CLIENT
Kent Hoskins

COLLABORATORS
Sheppard Construction (contractor); Fine Line Aluminium (supplier)

TOTAL SURFACE AREA
1,991.3 sq ft

PHOTOGRAPHY
© Paul McAneary Architects

As the result of a 30° shift in the floor plan, this home
provides several different yet thoroughly unique views.

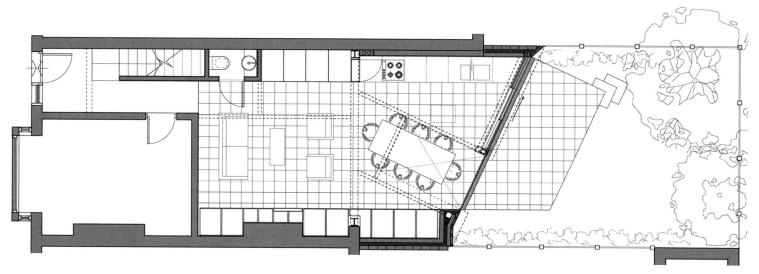

Plan

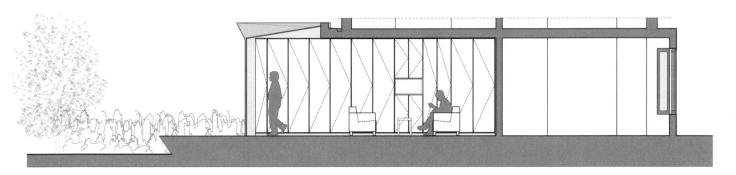

Section A-A

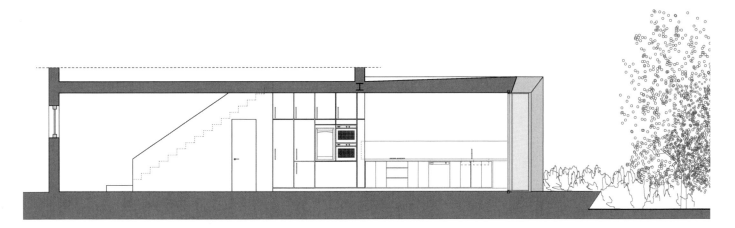

Section B-B

KONA RESIDENCE

Kona, HI, USA 2010

The Kona Residence is located in Hawaii. More precisely, this modern home is positioned between two extremely different natural landscapes: the volcanic mountain chain and the ocean. Surprisingly, the geometric-style architecture blends harmoniously with the lush natural surroundings.

Innovatively designed, this residence is arranged as a series of pods distributed throughout the building. To create these pods, steel tubes, also referred to as sheaths, are introduced into the terrain, and provide the rigidity needed to form a concrete column. This system is generally laid out as a series of environments that serve as the residence's common areas. An external gallery corridor functions as a central axis that connects all the pods.

The house is characterized by its relationship with the surrounding natural environment. Two separate arrays of photovoltaic panels are located on the roof. This roof offsets energy use in the home. In a similar strategy, darker lava stone lines the pool; this stone helps heat the water through solar radiation. Finally, three dry wells recycle rainwater and supply the house with water.

ARCHITECT
Belzberg Architects

COLLABORATORS
Hagy Belzberg (principal); Barry Gartin (project manager); David Cheung, Barry Gartin, Cory Taylor, Andrew Atwood, Christ Arntzen, Brock DeSmit, Dan Rentsch, Lauren Zuzack, Justin Brechtel, Phillip Lee, Aaron Leppanen (project team); William Blankeney Inc (structural consultant); Mark Morrison & Associates (mechanical consultant); Tinguely Development (general contractor), MLK Studio (interior designer); Belt Collins Hawaii, Joe Roderick Hawaiian Landscapes Inc (landscape designer)

TOTAL SURFACE AREA
7,800 sq ft

PHOTOGRAPHY
© Benny Chan/Fotoworks, Belzberg Architects

The Kona Residence is comprised of a series of
pods. It also features locally sourced materials,
such as native wood and dark lava stone.

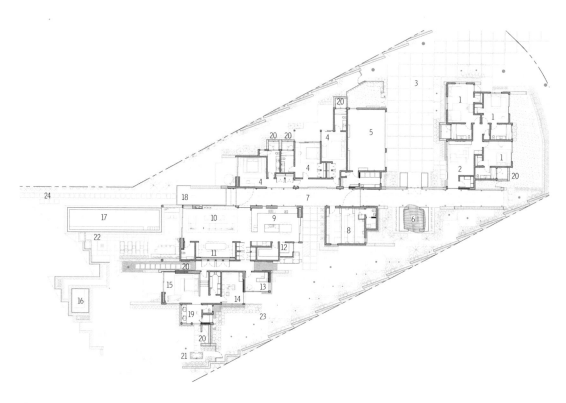

Plan

1. Kids' bedroom
2. Kids' common room
3. Motor court
4. Guest room
5. Garage
6. Entry pavilion
7. Outdoor gallery
8. Theater
9. Kitchen
10. Lounge
11. Dining room
12. Office 1
13. Office 2
14. Gym
15. Master bedroom
16. Hot tub
17. Pool
18. Reflecting pool
19. Master bathroom
20. Outdoor shower
21. Outdoor tub
22. Conversation pit
23. Fruit grove
24. Pineapple patch

440

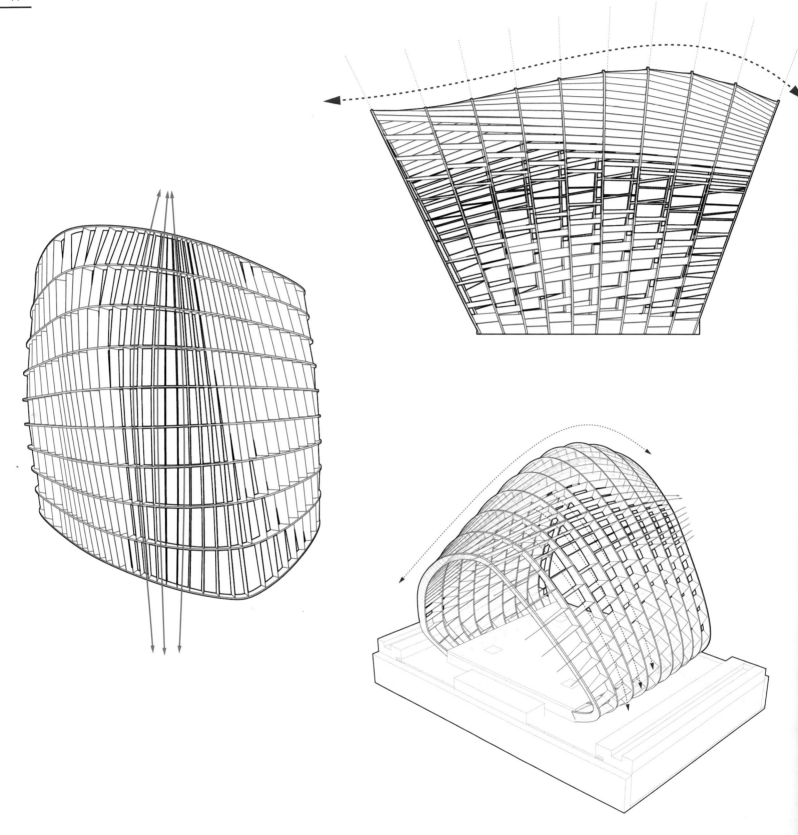

Constructive diagrams

BRENTWOOD RESIDENCE

Los Angeles, CA, USA   2007

While this Brentwood residence is located at the foot of California's Santa Monica Mountains, it nonetheless did not offer any picturesque views of the surroundings. To overcome this obstacle, the architects focused their attention on working within the physical limits of the property. To this end, the team made use of the existence of a large California oak at the back of the site. This tree became the focal point of the formal parts of this project. The architects played with the idea of formality and informality by drawing an imaginary line down the blueprint, thus separating the main formal reception room from the various informal spaces.

The exterior of the building is modern in tone. Its façade is a series of asymmetric volumes that feature a complex interlocking geometry. The interior design makes abundant use of materials from the mid-twentieth century—plaster, Pennsylvania bluestone veneers and facings, and Mangaris hardwood paneling. The result is classic design from the outside in.

ARCHITECT
Belzberg Architects

COLLABORATORS
Hagy Belzberg (principal); Daniel Rentsch (project manager); David Cheung, Barry Gartin, Brock DeSmit, Justin Brechtel, Ryan Thomas, Eric Stimmel, Erik Sollom, Brad Lang (project team); Risha Engineering (structural consultant); John Dorius & Associates (mechanical consultant); Group F Builders (general contractor), Meg Joannides/MI K Studio (interior designer); Knibb Design (landscape designer)

TOTAL SURFACE AREA
12,083 sq ft

PHOTOGRAPHY
© Art Gray Photography, Benny Chan/ Fotoworks

The interior of the home features elements and
décor typical of mid-twentiethcentury design.

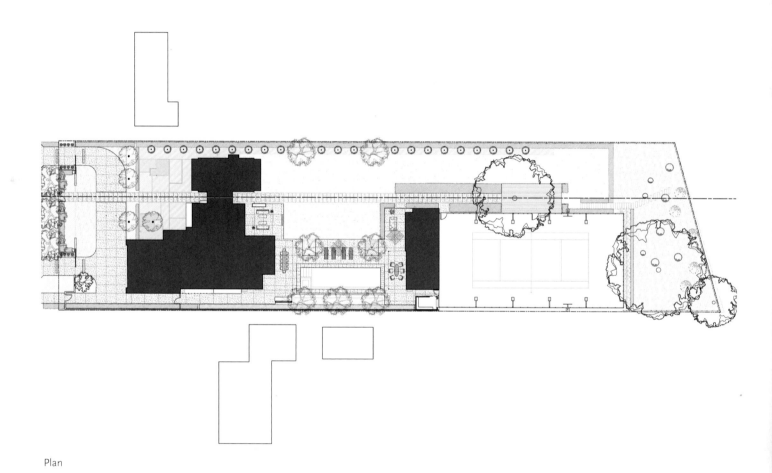

Plan

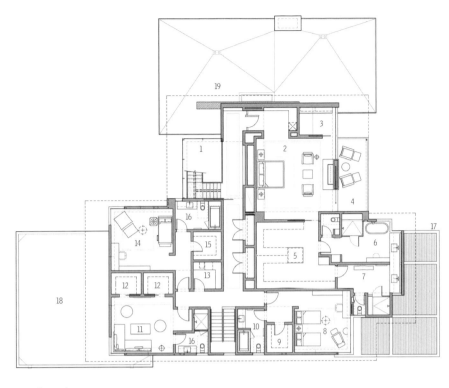

First floor plan

1. Main staircase
2. Master bedroom
3. Studio
4. Covered deck
5. Wardrobe 1
6. Master bathroom (hers)
7. Master bathroom (his)
8. Bedroom 1
9. Wardrobe 2
10. Bathroom 1
11. Media room
12. Storage room
13. Utility room
14. Bedroom 2
15. Wardrobe 3
16. Bathroom 2
17. Trellis (below)
18. Roof 1 (below)
19. Roof 2 (below)

Ground floor plan

1. Living room
2. Main entry
3. Formal dining
4. Kitchen
5. Pantry
6. Powder room 1
7. Family room
8. Breakfast area
9. Office
10. Powder room 2
11. Bathroom
12. Bedroom
13. Mud room
14. Utility room
15. Garage
16. Outdoor living room
17. Outdoor dining room

The home is characterized by a clear division between the formal and the informal spaces. An imaginary dividing line, drawn down the length of the layout, clearly separates both areas.

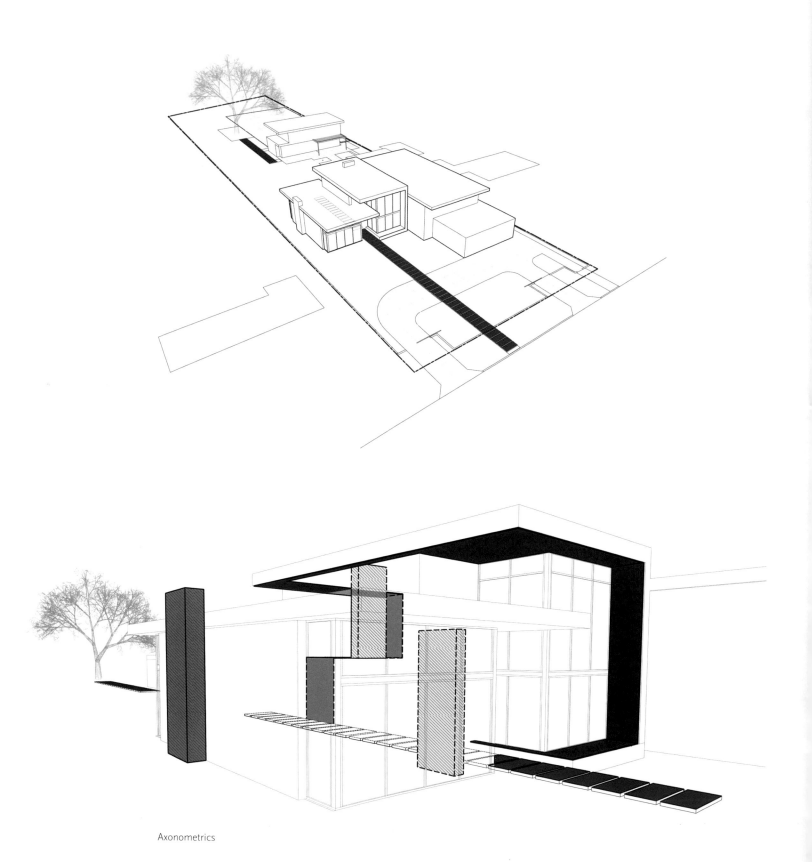

Axonometrics

BLACK & WHITE HOUSE

Yarmouk, Kuwait   2009

This residential complex is comprised of six individual villas with interior spaces formed by rectangular prisms. The villas are accessed from a single street but face two different directions. Those located at the front of the complex are raised 7 ft (2 m) over the street level and are accessible from the main street. The villas surround private courtyards that offer respite. The three villas located at the rear of the complex are more complex and linear in shape. Their design is comprised of a series of voids that face outward and open to the street. Each villa is ample in space and has four bedrooms and three living areas further complemented by a kitchen, a garage, and a service area. All the buildings make use of stone and stucco as finishing materials. This creates homogeneity and unifies the complex as a single structure.

ARCHITECT
Nasser Abulhasan, Joaquín Pérez Goicoechea/AGi Architects

COLLABORATORS
Georg Thesing, Sharifah Alshalfan, Germana DeDonno, Nasseba Shaji, Lucía Sánchez Salmón, Robert A. Varghese, Moyra Montoya Moyano, Bruno Afonso Martins Gomes (project team); AMJT (consultant)

TOTAL SURFACE AREA
36,759 sq ft

COST
$4,195,951

PHOTOGRAPHY
© Nelson Garrido

One of the most characteristic aspects of this
project is the color contrast of the façades:
black and white to define the individuality of this
home. The structure is not a solid block, but
a labyrinth of interior and exterior spaces.

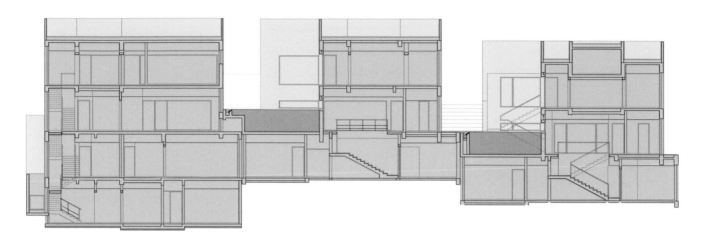

Section

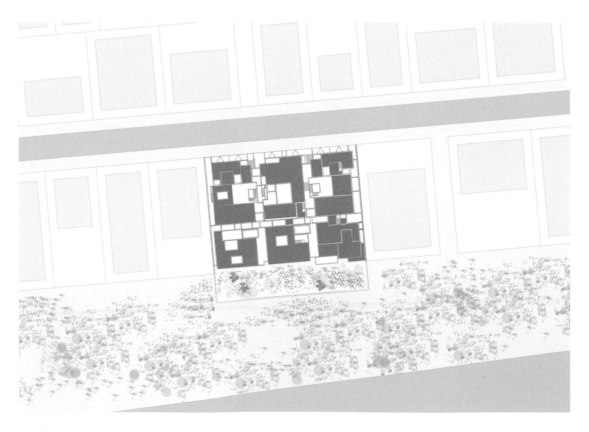

Site plan

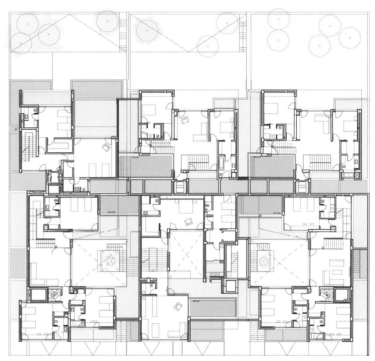

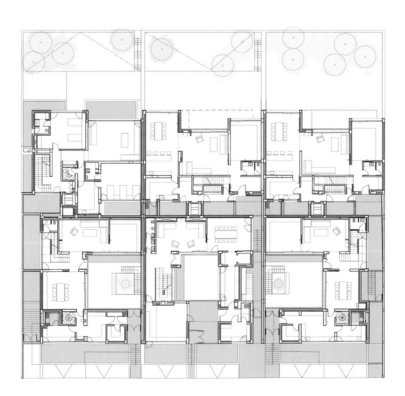

Plans

GAP HOUSE

London, United Kingdom   2007

This house is located in a London neighborhood. Its most striking feature is its width. The residence stands on a lot measuring only 8 ft (2.3 m) across in a West London conservation area.

With a street frontage of this width, the house is literally fitted into a slot. The challenge faced with this project was that of creating a low-carbon building and a four-bedroom home that offered abundant daylight and space on such a narrow site. To achieve this, the architects placed the bedrooms at the front of the house and left storage areas at the rear. A courtyard also located at the rear of the house is both an open-air space and a source of light. A central staircase connects the different floors.

The house incorporates a series of green strategies, including passive solar gain, high levels of insulation, a ground-coupled heat pump, and rainwater harvesting. In this way, it achieves energy savings of approximately 30 percent compared to a house built using typical construction standards.

ARCHITECT
Pitman Tozer Architects

CLIENT
Luke Tozer

COLLABORATORS
Nurture Nature (landscape);
Briary Energy (energy);
Brownstone Ltd (general contractor)

TOTAL SURFACE AREA
1,991.3 sq ft

PHOTOGRAPHY
© Nick Kane

The house is located on a narrow lot. In order to make best use of this peculiar feature and to increase light capture, the bedrooms are laid out at the front of the house while storage areas are located at the rear.

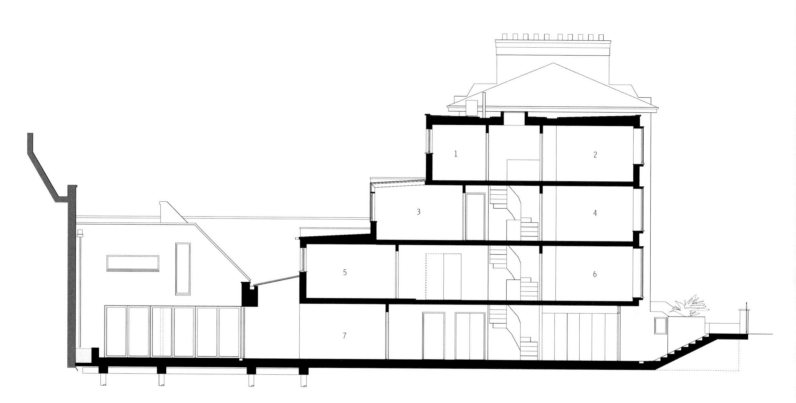

Section A-A

1. Bathroom
2. Bedroom 4
3. Conservatory
4. Bedroom 3
5. Bedroom 1
6. Bedroom 2
7. Kitchen

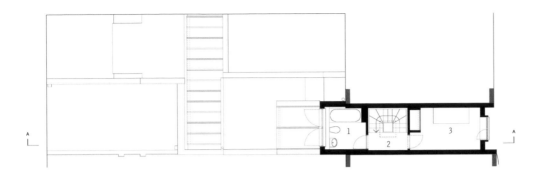

Third floor plan

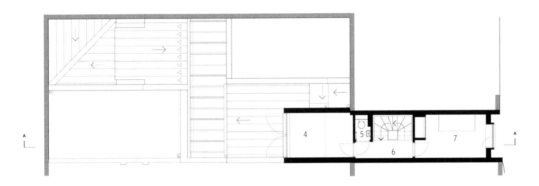

Second floor plan

1. Bathroom 1
2. Hall 1
3. Bedroom 4
4. Conservatory
5. Toilet
6. Hall 2
7. Bedroom 3
8. Studio
9. Bedroom 1
10. Bathroom 2
11. Hall 3
12. Bedroom 2
13. Living room
14. Courtyard
15. Dining room
16. Kitchen
17. Utility room
18. Heat pump
19. Hall 3

First floor plan

Ground floor plan

18 CAVENDISH AVENUE

Cambridge, United Kingdom   2008

To create this home, the team proposed a building that would showcase exemplary quality of design, scale, and construction, while reinforcing and improving the quality of the already-existing architecture of the street. Local planning authorities were consulted to make sure the plans didn't violate the architectural codes of the historic neighborhood. The orientation is in line with the design, with the north-south axis of the site allowing good use to be made of daylight. The south façade, facing the garden, was designed to give predominance to the views. Protection from the sun is provided by a screen of wood shutters. North-facing openings are limited to three windows, with one large one over the living area and the central staircase. The street façade features semi-reflective frosted glass as cladding and protection from the rain, reflecting the sky at the same time.

The street frontage for the lower level and one projection room is clad in wood. The upper two levels are clad in a somewhat opaque semi-reflective glass, which avoids appearing too corporate through the use of small panes that provide a sense of delicateness. The rear first and second floor façades consist of sliding glass panels.

ARCHITECT
Mole Architects

COLLABORATORS
Cambridge Building Company (contractor); WitbyBird (engineer); Sheriff Tiplady (quantity surveyor)

TOTAL SURFACE AREA
2,207 sq ft

COST
$927,876

PHOTOGRAPHY
© Mole Architects

This project is located in a suburb with a wide variety of architectural styles, featuring large houses and an interesting street with detached frontages. The design replaces a 1930s family home with a contemporary building.

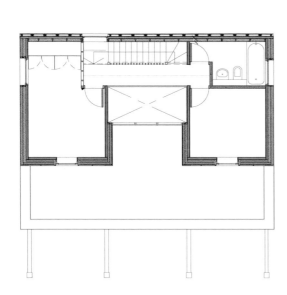

Second floor plan

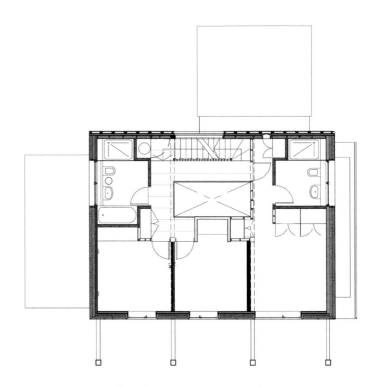

First floor plan

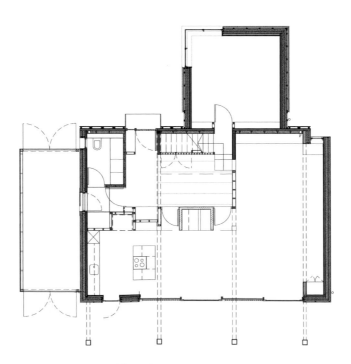

Ground floor plan

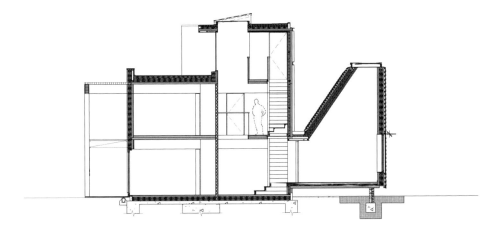

North-south section

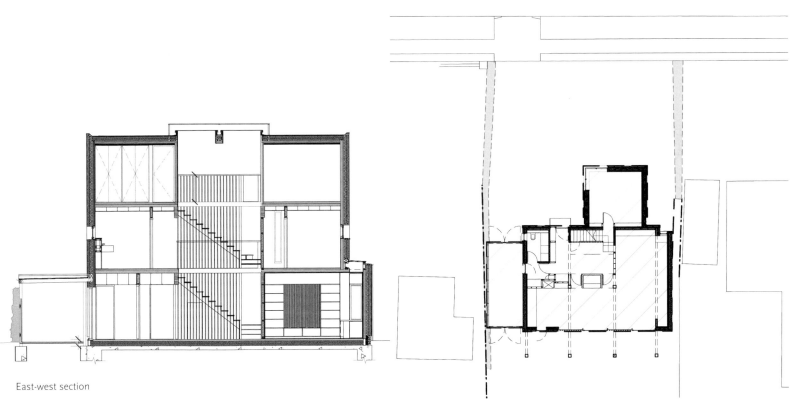

East-west section

Site plan

HONIGHAUS

San Francisco, CA, USA   2009

This project is an interior remodeling and enlargement of a penthouse that offers views of the Golden Gate Bridge and Alcatraz. Architecturally, it illustrates a common dilemma specific to the architecture of San Francisco. The design emerged from the tension between the homeowners' wishes for a contemporary dwelling in the city and the traditional planning rules set by the San Francisco Planning Department, in this case with reference to the homes in the Pacific Heights neighborhood.

The original building dates from 1910 and has been remodeled several times during the past century. The façade was restored to its original Edwardian austerity and painted gray. The roof was redesigned and covered with copper as a complement to the gray façade. This provides a calm and unified exterior aspect that participates innocently in the fabric of façades on the street.

The interior space was restructured with a geometric transformation that extends to the main transit ways, with a confluence from the entrance to the exterior, more emphatically onto the terrace. Although the residence had been remodeled several times, the style of many of the main rooms was kept, to contrast with the fluid geometries of the main transit area. The more traditional spaces were interpreted through different means of ornamentation and feature a wealth of materials. The solidness of the original building evaporates in the penthouse, where the walls and ceilings offer panoramic views over San Francisco Bay and the Presidio.

ARCHITECT
Ogrydziak/Prillinger Architects

COLLABORATORS
Luke O'Gryzdiak, Zoë Prillinger, Leo Henke, Haemi Chang, Gisela Schmoll (project team); Santos + Urrutia (structural engineer); Webb Construction (general contractor)

TOTAL SURFACE AREA
3,504 sq ft

PHOTOGRAPHY
© Prillinger Architects

The solidness of this project is the result
of using materials like plaster, stone, steel,
ceramic, glass, mirrors, and upholstered
panels in the different rooms, in addition to a
rigorous selection of finishes and décor.

478

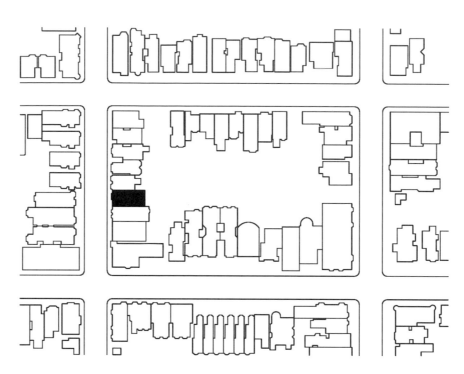

Site plan

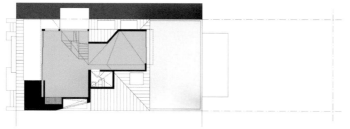

Third floor plan

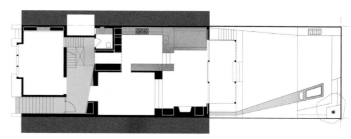

First floor plan

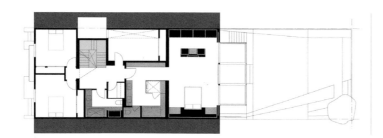

Second floor plan

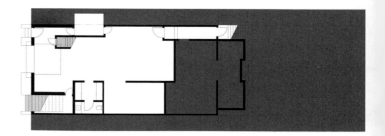

Garage plan

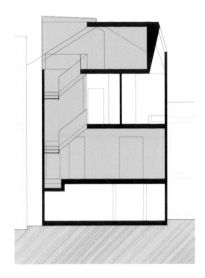

Cross section

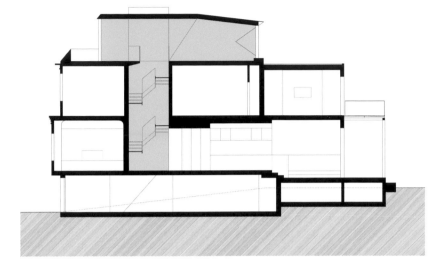

Longitudinal section

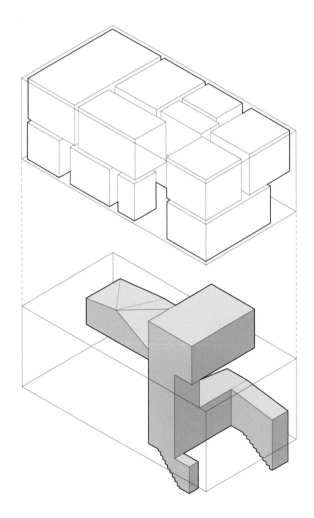

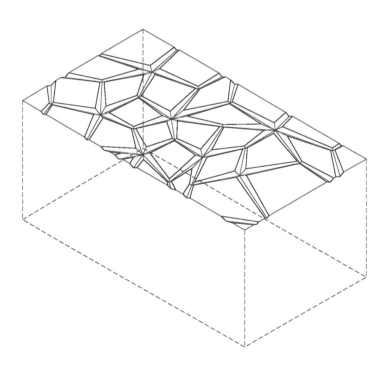

Diagrams

FAMILIA HOUSE

San Diego, CA, USA   2008

The aim of this project was to design and build an energy-efficient house that used active and passive strategies to lower the need for energy, water, and resources. It also involved creating a modern and comfortable home for a young family of six.

The home makes use of several passive low-cost lifestyle strategies. It uses 65 percent less electricity than national standards and 55 percent less water compared to other households, without cutting back on comfort or aesthetics. The design itself consists of a large two-story rectangular prism, which provides 100 percent natural ventilation. The lengthwise positioning of the house in an east-west direction provides maximum access to natural light.

The north façade features a variety of window types, while the south and west sides, with their few openings, are more exposed to the heat. Wide eaves of up to 8 ft (92.5 m) cover and protect the window openings. Large trees were planted in order to provide more shade.

The house dramatically increases its efficiency through the use of new technologies, such as sensors that turn off lights when part of the house is unoccupied. Water is heated by two solar panels on a 90-gallon tank for both domestic use and radiant heating.

ARCHITECT
Kevin deFreitas Architects

COLLABORATORS
Manish Desai (design team); Leslie Ryan (landscape architect); Alex Barajas (structural engineer); Lightworks (lighting designer)

TOTAL SURFACE AREA
3,460 sq ft

PHOTOGRAPHY
© Harrison Photographic

This modern and comfortable home
is perfect for a large family.

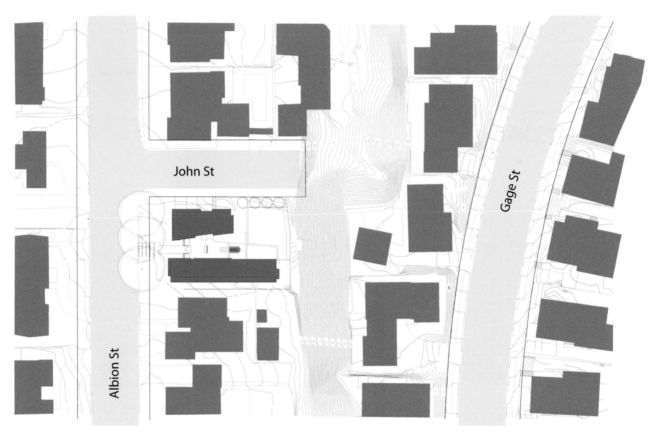

Site plan

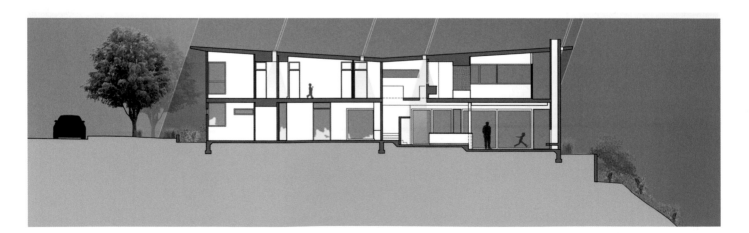

Section

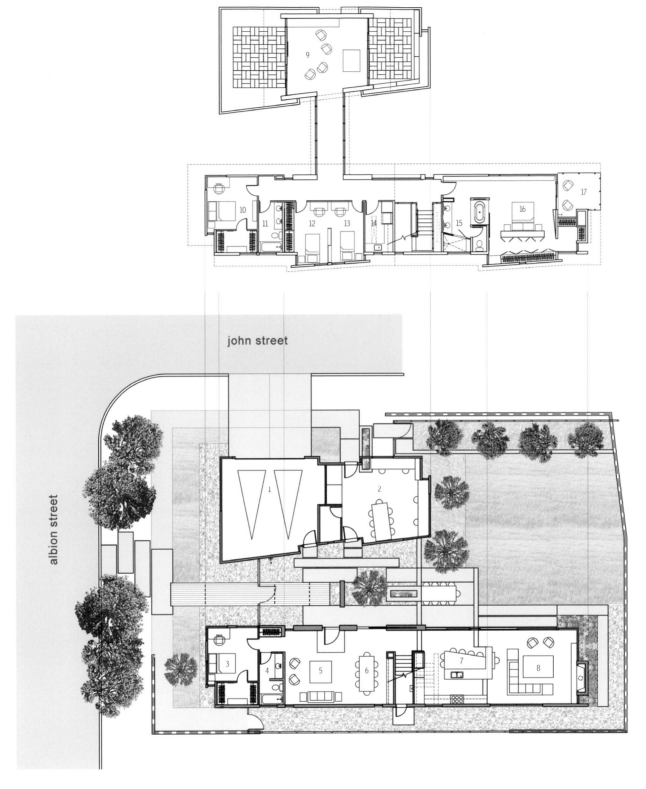

john street

albion street

Floor plans

1. Garage
2. Office
3. Bedroom 1
4. Bathroom 1
5. Family room
6. Dining room
7. Kitchen
8. Living room
9. Playroom
10. Bedroom 2
11. Bathroom 2
12. Shared bedroom
13. Shared bedroom
14. Laundry room
15. Master bathroom
16. Master bedroom
17. Master balcony

FAIRWAYS RESIDENCE

Nashville, TN, USA   2000

The premise behind this residence, located in Nashville, Tennessee, was the exploration of the relationship between nature and architecture. To this end, the team created a man-made border—or dividing line—between the home's public and private spaces. The rear façade is transparent, and provides a direct connection between the interior spaces and the protected natural order of the courtyard. The transparency also lets lots of natural light fall into the house.

The project is part of a gated community bordering a golf course, which divides the area into three distinct communities. The convergence between urban order and the natural setting influenced by the dryness of the desert has resulted in a villa that unites these two very different realms. In the particular case of this residence, the limits established between the interior and exterior spaces are formed by different materials, such as stone, concrete, and glass.

The entrance to the site is formed by a clearing edged by the stone wall that is the limit between the house and garden.

ARCHITECT
Eric Rosen Architects

COLLABORATORS
Eric Rosen (principal); Veit Kugel, Bob Hsin (project team); Carrie Jordan, Chris Hope, Robert Casserly (project assistant); Phillip White/Phillip White Engineering (structural engineer); Duncan Calicott/Calicott and Associates (landscape architect); Tom Bulla/ Bulla Associates Architects (project representative); Wayne Hilton/The Hilton Company (general contractor)

TOTAL SURFACE AREA
6,800 sq ft

PHOTOGRAPHY
© Erich Koyama

This home plays with the idea of limits.
Attention is drawn to the frontier between
public and private spaces and between
nature and a man-made urban setting.

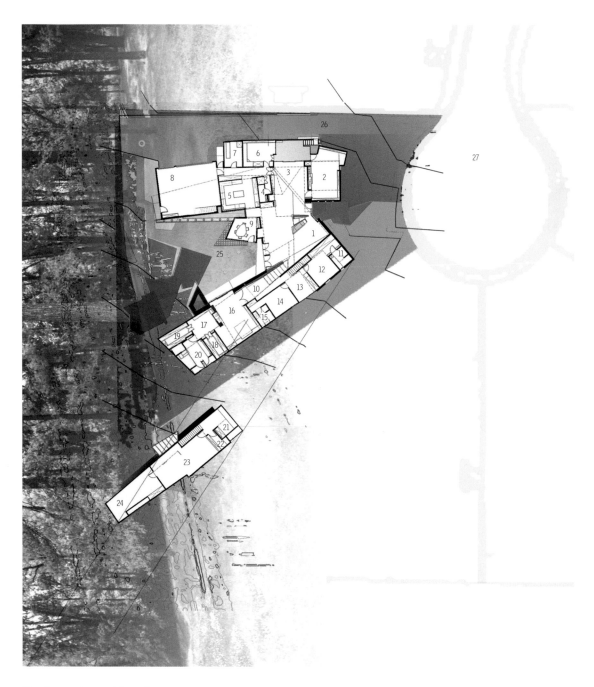

First floor and ground floor plan

1. Great room
2. Library
3. Dining room
4. Powder room
5. Kitchen
6. Office
7. Laundry room
8. Garage
9. Breakfast room
10. Gallery
11. Guest bath 1
12. Guest bedroom 1
13. Sitting room
14. Guest bedroom 2
15. Guest bath 1
16. Master bedroom
17. Dressing room
18. Closet 1
19. Closet 2
20. Master bath
21. Sewing room
22. Sewing room storage
23. Fitness room
24. Storage room
25. Courthyard
26. Driveway
27. Cul de sac

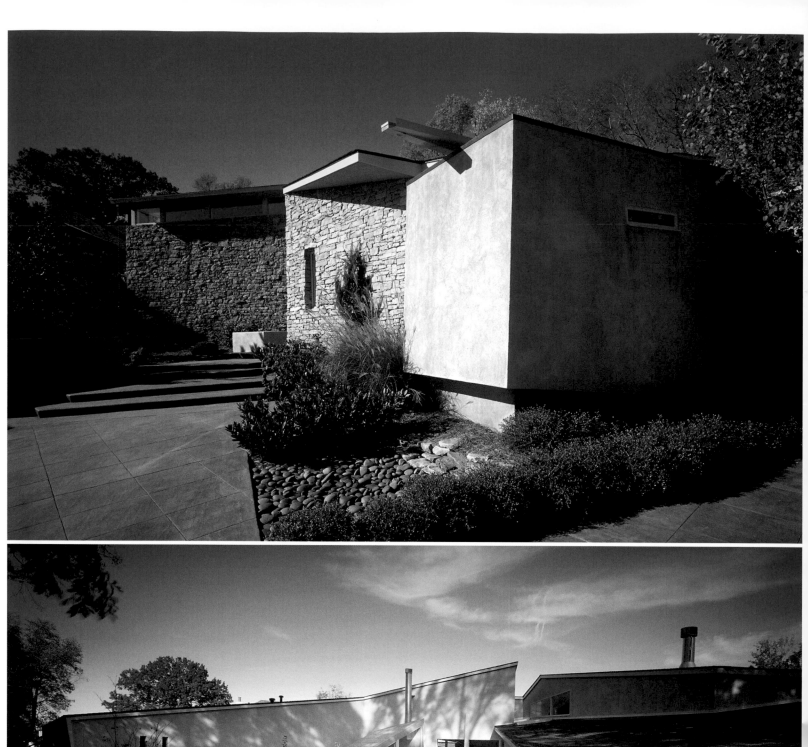

Rendered section

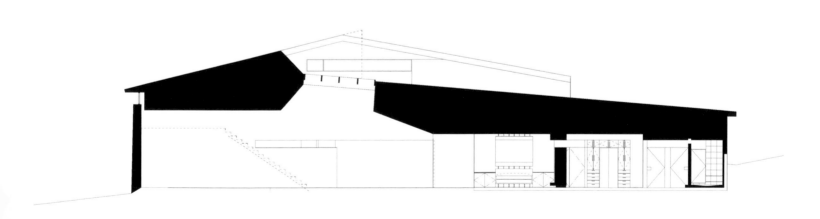

Section

DAVIDSON RESIDENCE

Seattle, WA, USA   2010

This rebuilt house, located in Seattle, Washington, made use of the pre-existing foundations on the site. The design program sought to maximize both the surface area of the site and the views.

The home is laid out as a series of different volumes defined by the materials used to clad them. The bamboo floors, for example, not only demarcate different spaces but also bring warmth to the interior design. Bamboo is also used on the upper level and the roof terrace. Other materials include wood, glass, and leather. The careful combination of these materials creates a unique space, one that is both singular and personal, and is able to retain a timeless design sensibility.

ARCHITECT
BUILD

CLIENT
Mike Davidson

COLLABORATORS
Swenson Say Fagét Structural Engineers (consultants)

TOTAL SURFACE AREA
4,500 sq ft

COST
$909,000

PHOTOGRAPHY
© BUILD

The home features large glazed expanses
that provide a fluid connection between
the interior and exterior spaces.

Site plan

Pre-existing house
Adjacent homes
Critical areas: steep slope
Maximum building area

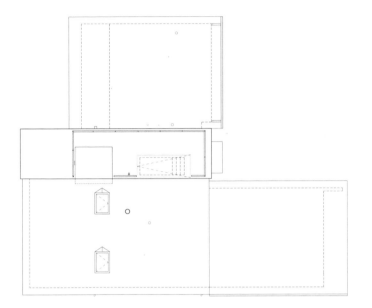

Roof plan

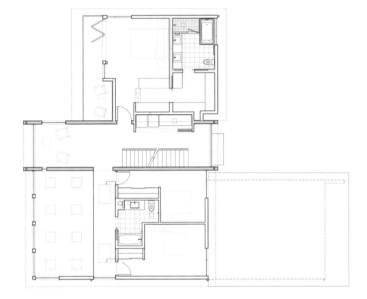

First floor plan

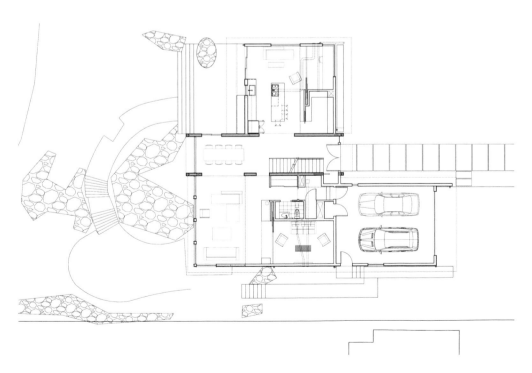

Ground floor plan

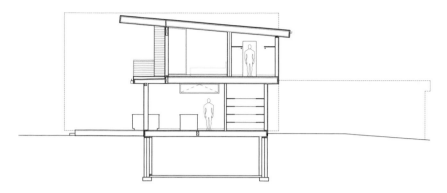

Kitchen and master suite section

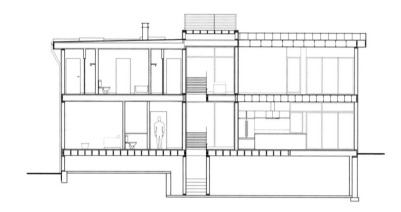

North-south section

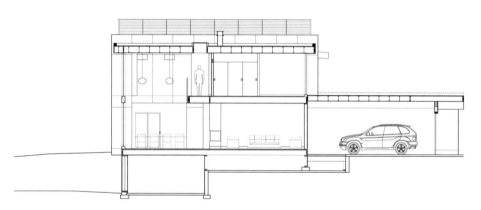

Living room and garage section

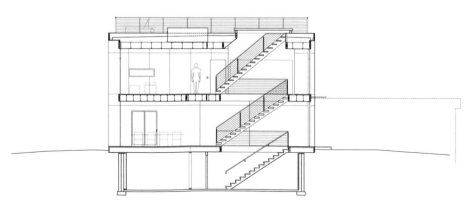

Circulation section

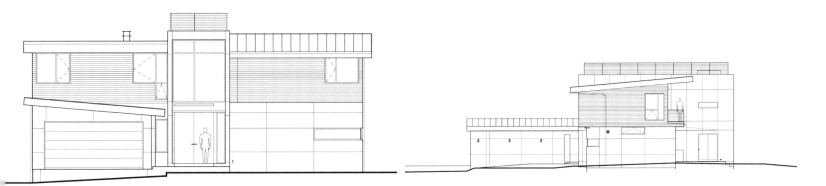

East elevation

North elevation

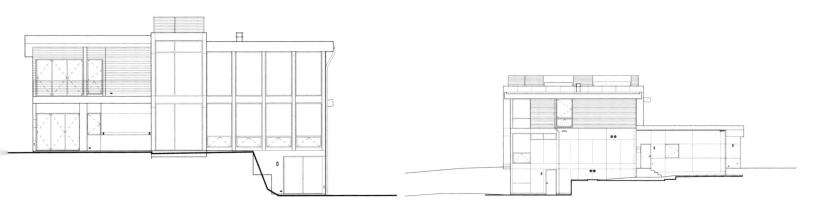

West elevation

South elevation

SANCTUARY COVE RESIDENCE

Gold Coast, QLD, Australia   2007

This residence is located in the middle of an island. It features impressive views of a distant golf course without compromising any of its occupants' privacy.

This structure has been pared down to a minimum of materials and construction elements. Structurally, the residence is a series of planes in walls and roof that extend into the surrounding landscape. The roof is generally flat, though it does slope north over the living area. The design features large bedrooms and public areas that are directly connected with the exterior.

The entrance is in the southeast corner of the site and is preceded by a leisure area. This comprises a clear pavilion and a terrace with views over a golf course. This transparent pavilion connects the two wings of the house. One of these houses the private rooms, while the other contains the public spaces. The former consists of three bedrooms, each with private bathrooms, and the master bedroom with its en suite bathroom. It also has a large closet and ample views of the golf course and garden. The public area comprises the living/dining area with stone fireplace and the kitchen. There is an adjoining wet room with an exit to the street.

The patio of the residence is designed to provide views of the golf course. It also features ecologically responsible design, enabling it to provide a natural ventilation system.

ARCHITECT
Adam Beck, Steve McCracken, Erica Borgstrom/BDA Architecture

TOTAL SURFACE AREA
7,534.7 sq ft

PHOTOGRAPHY
© David Sandison Photography

This house is simply designed and built. Its
sophistication comes from the careful blend of
tradition and modern styles in its décor and the
striking views of a neighboring golf course.

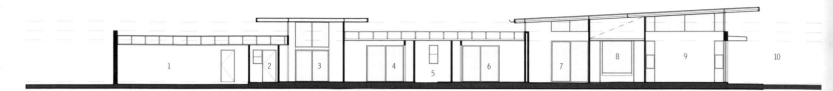

Section D-D

1. Garage 1   6. Bedroom 2
2. Laundry room   7. Ensuite bahtroom 2
3. Office   8. Dressing room
4. Bedroom 1/gym   9. Master bedroom
5. Ensuite bahtroom 1   10. Terrace 1

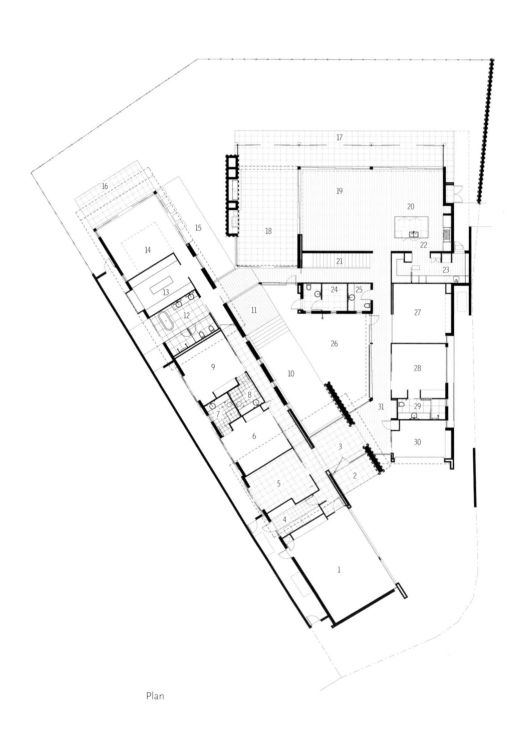

Plan

1. Garage 1
2. Entry and terrace
3. Entry
4. Laundry room
5. Office
6. Bedroom 1/gym
7. Ensuite bahtroom 1
8. Ensuite bahtroom 3
9. Bedroom 2
10. Pool
11. Deck
12. Ensuite bahtroom 2
13. Dressing room
14. Master bedroom
15. Reflection pond
16. Terrace 2
17. Terrace 1
18. Screened porch
19. Living room
20. Dining room
21. Sitting area
22. Kitchen
23. Scullery
24. Pool equipment
25. Powder room
26. Central courtyard
27. Media room
28. Guest room
29. Ensuite bahtroom 4
30. Garage 2
31. Gallery

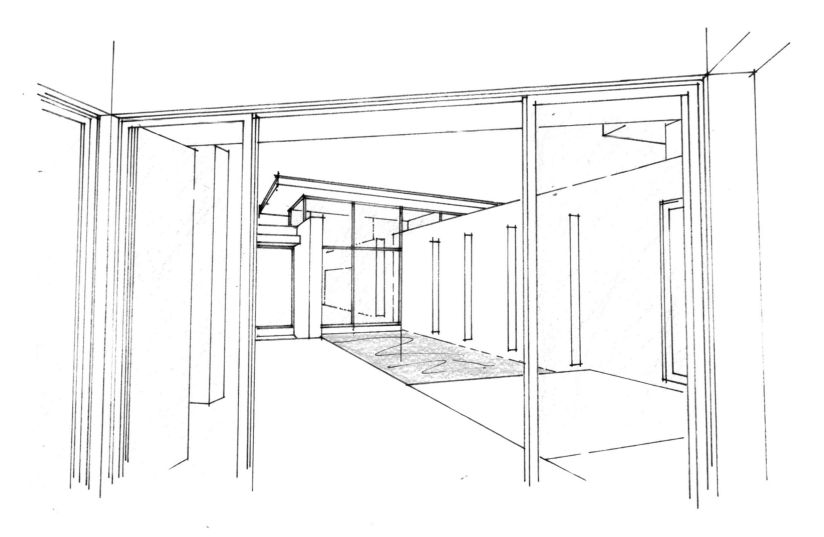

Perspective sketch

MONTECITO RESIDENCE

Montecito, CA, USA   2010

As its name indicates, the Montecito Residence is located in Montecito, California. This part of the world is an ecologically sensitive habitat with thick plant cover and large rocks.

The program for the home included a main house, a garage, and a swimming pool with pool house. The main residence is divided into two wings. One of these contains the public spaces of living room and kitchen, while the other contains the private spaces of bedrooms, bathrooms, and library. All the rooms in the latter have a direct connection to the exterior, either through small patios or terraces.

The design of this home fulfills several prerequisites, such as blending in with the landscape, responding to the program of the occupants' needs, and being ecologically sustainable. To comply with the last function, mostly glass and steel were used. The steel was recycled from car bodies, making it a "green" material.

The house has little need for air-conditioning, as it is cooled almost exclusively by cross ventilation. This system is enhanced by the use of glass Dutch doors, sliding doors, and windows. All these elements help to adapt the climatic conditions to the occupants' needs. Radiant underfloor heating is fed from solar thermal and photovoltaic panels and high-efficiency boilers.

ARCHITECT
Barton Myers Associates

COLLABORATORS
Barton Myers (principal-in-charge); Thomas Schneider (associate-in-charge); Yianna Bouyioukou (project architect); Wayne Thomas, Cheng Zhou, David Karp (project team); Rios Clementi Hale Studios (landscape architect); Norman J. Epstein (structural); AGME Engineers (mechanical & plumbing); Smith Engineering Associates (electrical), Simpson Gumpertz & Heger Inc (envelope consultant); Penfield & Smith (civil); Grover-Hollingsworth & Associates (geotechnical); Caputo Construction (contractor)

TOTAL SURFACE AREA
3,865 sq ft

PHOTOGRAPHY
© Jim Simmons

The Montecito Residence was built using ecologically
sustainable materials, like glass and steel.

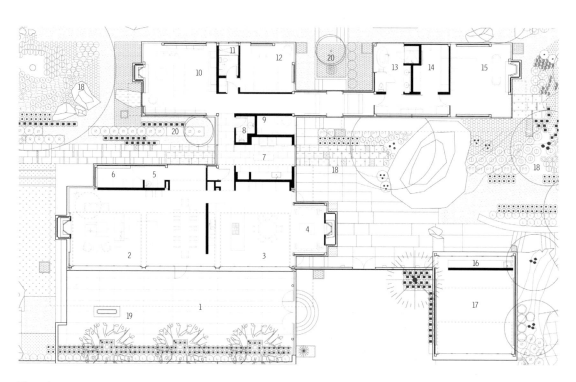

Floor plan

1. Terrace
2. Living/dining room
3. Kitchen
4. Reading room
5. Bar
6. Storage room
7. Pantry

8. Powder room
9. Mechanical room
10. Library
11. Guest bathroom
12. Guest bedroom
13. Master bathroom
14. Closet

15. Master bedroom
16. Garden room
17. Garage
18. Garden
19. Firepit
20. Fountain

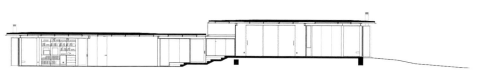

Library/hallway section

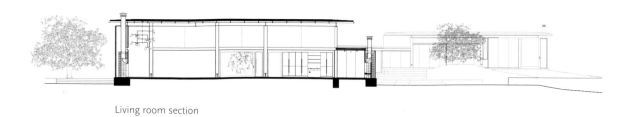

Living room section

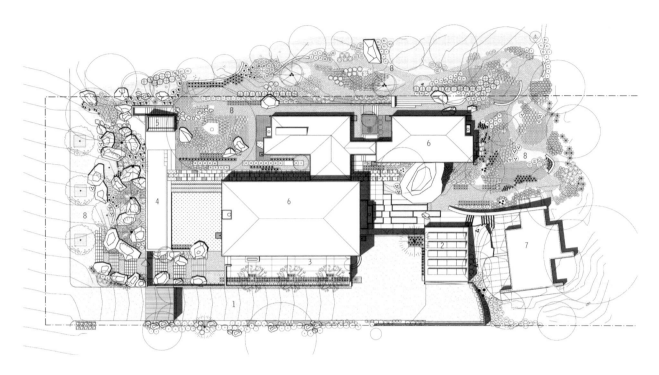

Site plan

1. Driveway
2. Garage
3. Terrace
4. Pool
5. Pergola
6. Main house
7. Guest house
8. Garden

South elevation

The interior décor features different pieces from
different styles coexisting to create a harmonious
atmosphere. As an example, custom-designed
furniture is combined with Asian and French
antiques, decorative rugs, and interior greenery.

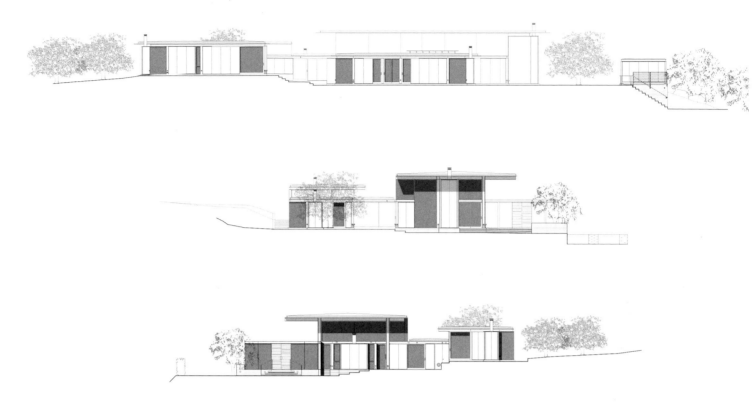

Noth, east and west elevations

Perspective sketch

MI-CA RESIDENCE

Los Angeles, CA, USA   2008

This residence is located in Los Angeles, California. This project is a thorough re-modeling of an existing building featuring Venetian stucco, a type of render that can make use of either natural or synthetic materials. The house was also enlarged by adding an extra floor.

The building was a series of dark, dis-ordered, and claustrophobic spaces. In order to change this situation, the team designed a two-story dwelling. This light-filled new home would have open-air spaces and offer panoramic views.

A series of sliding glass doors create a fluid dialogue between the interior and exterior spaces. As a result, the sliding door on the front corner of the lower level opens the house to the scenery created by the front garden and patio. The upper level has a similar door that offers excellent views from the back of the house. A large walnut staircase connects the two floors.

The interior design is the result of the architects working together with the client. This gave rise to a series of spaces with mixed textures and colors.

ARCHITECT
Jesse Bornstein,
Myungjong Lee/Bornarch

CLIENT
Chris Caris & Louise Mingenbach

COLLABORATORS
Scott Christiansen P.E. (structure);
L&D Group (HVAC)

TOTAL SURFACE AREA
2,731 sq ft

COST
$650,000

PHOTOGRAPHY
© Bernard Wolf

This remodeled and enlarged home was redesigned
to provide its interior with more daylight and
more points from which panoramic views could
be had. Different materials are featured in the
construction, including wood and Venetian stucco.

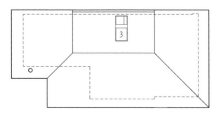

Roof plan

First floor plan

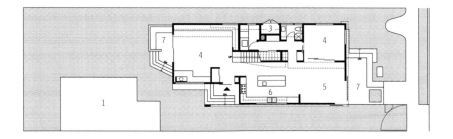

Ground floor plan

1. Garage
2. Bedroom
3. Service/mechanical room
4. Living room
5. Dining room
6. Kitchen
7. Outdoor living room

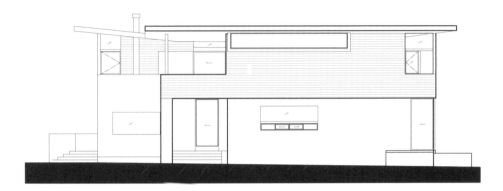

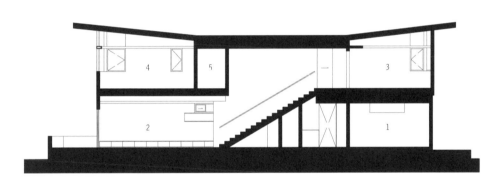

1. Guest bedroom
2. Living room
3. Bedroom
4. Master bedroom
5. Master closet
6. Dining room
7. Den

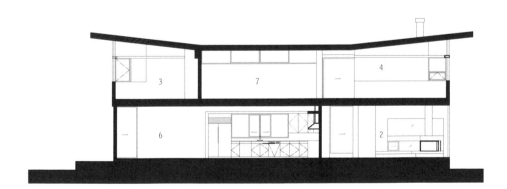

Elevation and sections

PANORAMA HOUSE

Santa Monica, CA, USA 2006

Located in the Ocean Park area of Santa Monica, California, this single-family home meets several criteria, one of which is the need to comply with local zoning laws that limit the building's height. Two strategies were implemented to respond to the surroundings and the building code, and to maximize the views and create a dynamic space. One of these strategies was the construction of a home with a program of volumes and a roof parallel with the slope of the terrain. The other strategy consisted of intensifying the horizontal nature of floor panels, viewing areas, and roof planes in order to provide indoor areas with more volume.

The borders between interior and exterior are blurred by a choice of materials and finishes, such as metal, brick, plaster, and wood that are common to both spaces. Vertical connections are present both outside and in. The former take the form of a bridge over the garden area that continues into the interior of the house like a spine connecting the different planes. The open internal staircase provides spatial interaction between the different levels. The living area, study, and children's rooms are examples of this connection between the different spaces.

There are also solar thermal and photovoltaic panels on the roof. The two sections of the roof covered by these panels slope toward the southwest, giving optimum orientation and enabling the best use to be made of them.

ARCHITECT
Jesse Bornstein,
Myungjong Lee/Bornarch

CLIENT
Shaun & Jesse Bornstein

COLLABORATORS
Parker-Resnick (structure); L&D Group Mechanical Eng. (HVAC); Golden Energy (solar); Energy Development Company (radiant floor system)

TOTAL SURFACE AREA
4,385 sq ft

COST
$1,200,000

PHOTOGRAPHY
© Bernard Wolf, Tom Bonner

The exterior of the home has a staircase over an area of the xeriscaped garden, which needs little water or maintenance. Other ecological features include a solar-heated swimming pool and a natural ventilation system.

544

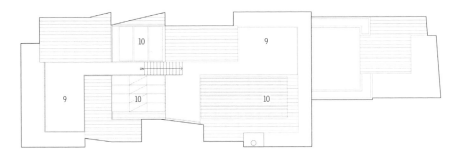

Roof plan

1. Studio
2. Garage
3. Water feature
4. Service/mechanical room
5. Bedroom
6. Living room
7. Dining room
8. Kitchen
9. Outdoor living room
10. Solar panels

First floor plan

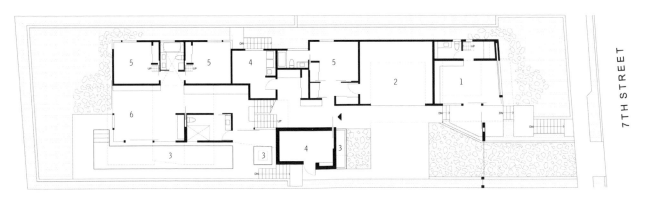

Ground floor plan

7TH STREET

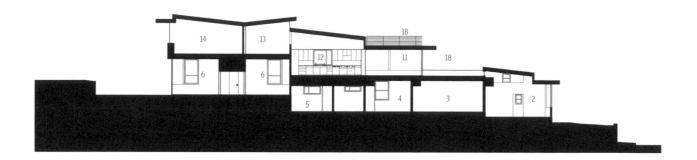

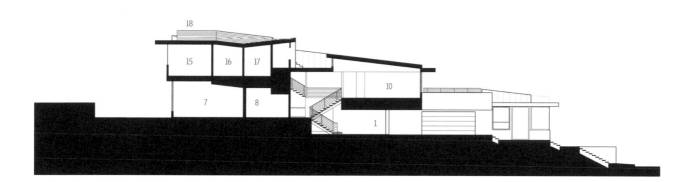

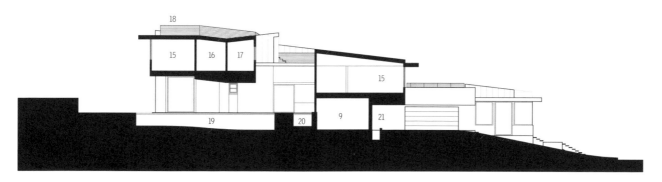

Sections

1.	Entry	12.	Kitchen
2.	Studio	13.	Sitting area
3.	Garage	14.	Master bedroom
4.	Guest room	15.	Master bathroom
5.	Laundry room	16.	Master closet
6.	Bedroom	17.	Den
7.	Family room	18.	Roof deck
8.	Bathroom	19.	Lap pool
9.	Mechanical room	20.	Jacuzzi
10.	Living room	21.	Koi pond
11.	Dining room		

DR. H HOUSE

Vienna, Austria   2006

Built on difficult terrain with a steep slope on the south side of the site, this multi-story, single-family home is located on the outskirts of Vienna, Austria. A narrow pathway leads to the site, which is graced with a private garden and swimming pool. A beautifully designed staircase mirrors the steep natural slope found outdoors, furthering the design conversation between exterior and interior. Echoing this sensibility, the bedrooms have large floor-to-ceiling windows for fluid communication with the outside. The clarity of this design is reinforced through the use of simple materials, such as white plaster, wood, glass, and concrete.

The main floor, which contains the living area, is located at the edge of the slope. This space faces north to offer spectacular views of the nearby church and the Vienna Woods. The kitchen and dining area are located on the same floor.

There is a strong separation between public and private spaces; the bedrooms are not on the same level as the public areas.

ARCHITECT
Christian Heiss, Michael Thomas, Thomas Mayer/Atelier Heiss

COLLABORATORS
Beatrix Vogler (project leader); Michael Petschl, Roman Zupanc (project team)

TOTAL SURFACE AREA
4,036.5 sq ft

PHOTOGRAPHY
© Peter Burgstaller/Archive Atelier Heiss

The large floor-to-ceiling windows provide
magnificent views and lots of natural light. The
white interiors make the space feel light and airy.

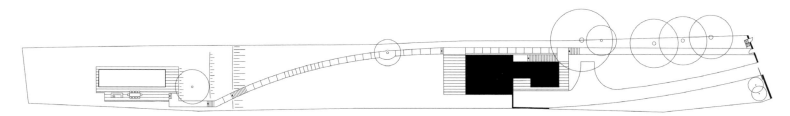

Site plan

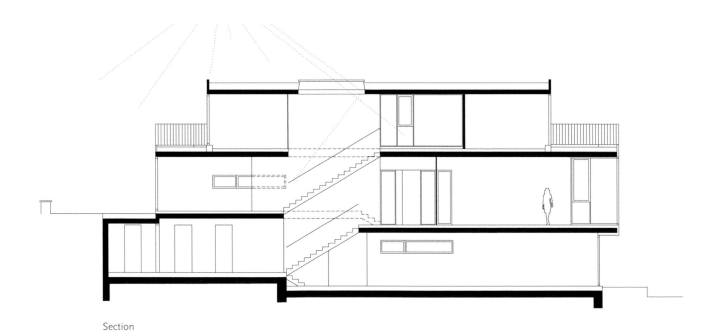

Section

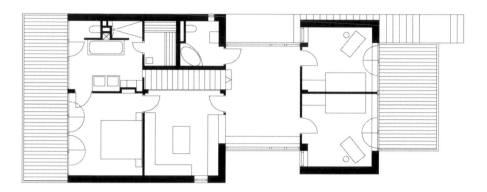

Second floor plan

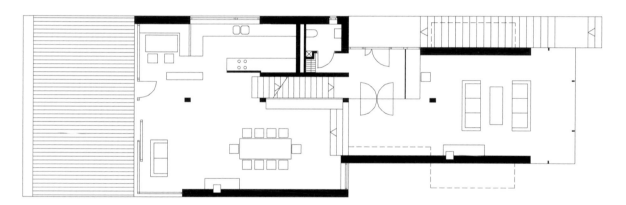

First floor plan

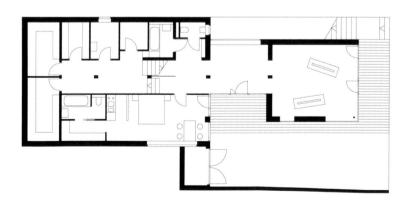

Ground floor plan

S HOUSE

Vienna, Austria   2007

This single-family home is the result of a thorough remodeling. In an effort to keep an element of the original home, the owners retained the old façade facing the street. The façade is of a style from a century before while the new architecture is thoroughly modern. This juxtaposition of form is both harmonious and unexpected, the perfect synthesis of seemingly opposing styles. Spacious balconies extend the interior outside, and floor-to-ceiling windows provide the home with abundant daylight without compromising its owners' privacy. At the rear of the house is a swimming pool, extended by an expanse of deck decorated with lounge chairs and a modern outdoor furniture suite.

The interior has a spacious public area revolving around a light-filled living room, in addition to wood-floored bedrooms and a number of different service areas, including bathrooms for adults and children.

ARCHITECT
Christian Heiss, Michael Thomas, Thomas Mayer/Atelier Heiss

COLLABORATORS
Thomas Mayer (project leader); Michael Petschl, Beatrix Vogler, Judith Ehmer (project team)

TOTAL SURFACE AREA
4,499.3 sq ft

PHOTOGRAPHY
© Peter Burgstaller/Archive Atelier Heiss

The rear of the house is done in a contemporary
style and favors glazed expanses.

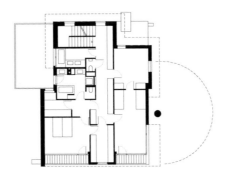

Third floor plan

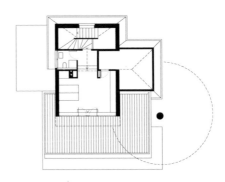

Second floor plan

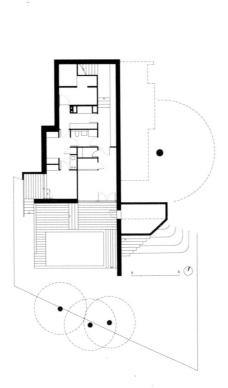

First floor plan

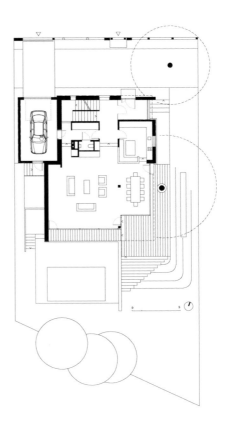

Ground floor plan

Perspective sketches

CS HOUSE

Guimarães, Portugal 2007

This project is located in the Portuguese city of Guimarães and is the result of a clear attempt to integrate the structure with the uneven topography typical of the terrain in this region. This three-story building is organized vertically as a solution to the problems that arose in the program.

One of the goals of the design was to establish connections between the home and its surroundings by blurring the boundaries between interior and exterior. All of the spaces feature terraces, either covered or open, that provide views of the landscape and open to them. The large openings were framed with a thick, white hollow structure. The roof is finished in exposed concrete. The entrance porch is in granite and the doorway is in polished marble, cement, and solid wood.

The third floor, located at street level, contains the entrance and garage. The second floor contains private spaces. The first floor houses the public areas, and offers integrated transit space with the garden and swimming pool.

ARCHITECT
Pitágoras Arquitectos

COLLABORATORS
Fernando Seara de Sá, Raul Roque Figueiredo, Alexandre Coelho Lima, Manuel Vilhena Roque (project team); Marlene Sousa, João Carvalho (collaborating architects); António Monteiro Castro, Sara Mourão/Projegui (engineering); Campos Marinho, João Araújo/CMA (mechanical engineering); Filipe Abreu/Apótema (electric engineering); Sociedade de Construções Guimar (general contractor)

TOTAL SURFACE AREA
8,611 sq ft

PHOTOGRAPHY
© João Ferrand

This house, organized to emphasize its verticality, consists of three floors: at street level is the second floor with the entrance and garage; underneath is the first floor reserved for the private areas; and finally the bottom floor, which houses the public areas.

Site plan

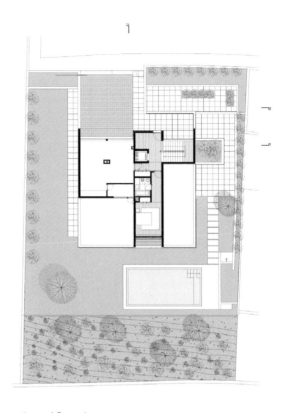

Second floor plan

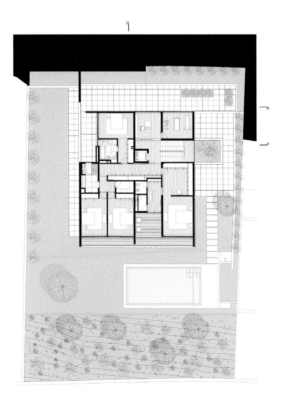

First floor plan

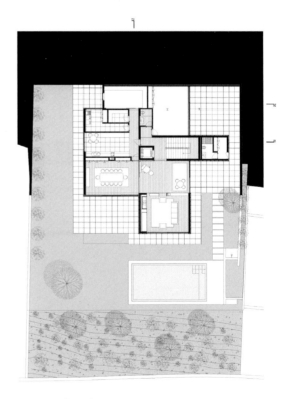

Ground floor plan

West elevation

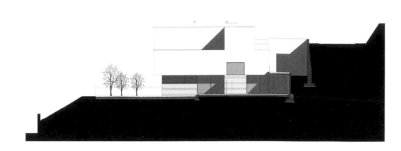

South elevation

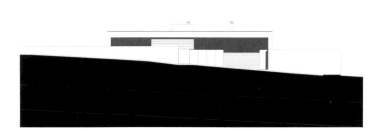

East elevation

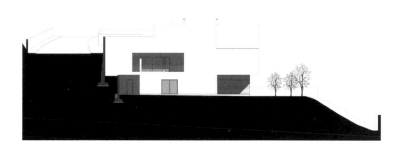

North elevation

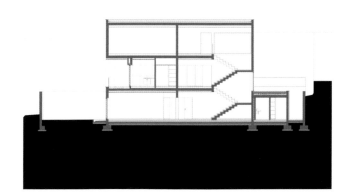

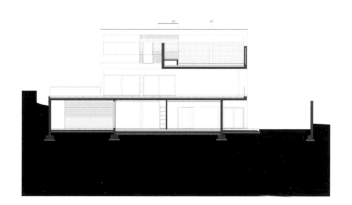

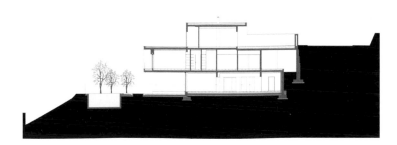

Sections

RESIDENCE IN NICOSIA

Nicosia, Cyprus   2004

Located on a small hill in the city of Nicosia, this home was built for a family of four. The slope provides an unobstructed view of Mount Pentadaktylos, rising above the eastern side of the city. The building is designed over three levels in order to adapt to the terrain and also to enhance the functional structure of the residence. The three levels follow the east-west axis of the sloping site. The south side contains only the uppermost level, containing the children's rooms. The living and dining areas are located on the intermediate level, which extends vertically to the ceiling, with a skylight through which abundant daylight penetrates the space. The lowest level contains the service and utility rooms and garage. The public spaces—the kitchen and living area—are on the second level, together with the main entrance to the house. The private space includes the bedrooms and a multipurpose office and is on the top floor. A semi-exterior space for rest and relaxation was built on the north side, bordering the swimming pool and enjoying mountain views.

On entering the residence, a window resembling a movie screen projects the external view of the city into the foyer. Once inside, those approaching the window are party to diverse and spectacular views.

ARCHITECT
Nikos Mesaritis, Marios Pelekanos/
Polytia Armos

CLIENT
Costas and Sofia Avraam

COLLABORATORS
Andreas Demitriades (building costs consultant); Giannos Zembylas (services engineer); Makis Ketonis (contractor); Nikos Kalathas (structural engineer)

TOTAL SURFACE AREA
5,382 sq ft

COST
$1,398,650

PHOTOGRAPHY
© Polytia Armos

Seen from the outside, the building expresses its composition as a series of three folds. The south-facing openings are limited to certain areas, while they increase in number and size toward the north.

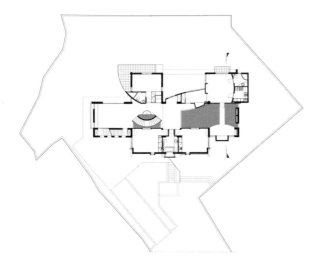

First floor plan

Ground floor plan

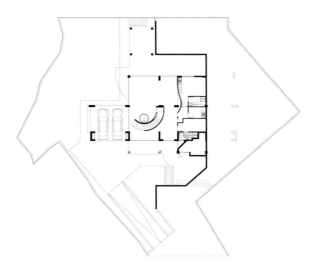

Basement plan

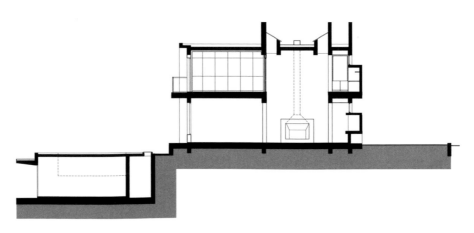

Section

TWO HOUSES AT ANIXI

Anixi, Greece   2009

Located on the outskirts of Athens, this project features two south-facing residences on a 10,760 sq ft (1,000 m²) lot. The aim and challenge of the design was to build two homes as a single entity, as one single project that brought unity and homogeneity to these two homes, united by identity and with a common basement and garden.

The program was based on the dissolving of boundaries between natural space and habitable space, for the purpose of unifying the interior spaces with the exterior. As the site was surrounded by vegetation, a way was sought to incorporate the spaces into the wooded setting. Panoramic vantage points were built through openings fitted into the metal roof.

The main structural element was a metal frame resting on concrete walls. This use of metal gave rise to a singular geometry. The galvanized roof and glass expanses form the façades. Both houses stand side by side with a hypsometric curve, guaranteeing privacy for each of the residences. Inside each of these, a concrete wall was used as a resource for the layout of spaces, with private spaces separated from public ones, and to connect both sides of the building.

ARCHITECT
React Architects

COLLABORATORS
Natasha Deliyianni (project manager); MFP Consulting Engineers (civil engineer); Gregoriades Dimitris (mechanical engineer)

TOTAL SURFACE AREA
8,611 sq ft

COST
$1,242,054

PHOTOGRAPHY
© Elias Handelis

Two homes conceived as one entity. With a
similar design, the shared garden unites them,
while the hypsometric curve from the roof
protects the privacy of each of the spaces.

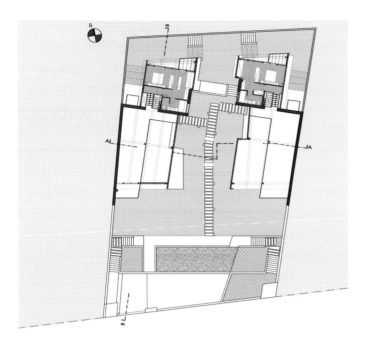

Second floor plan

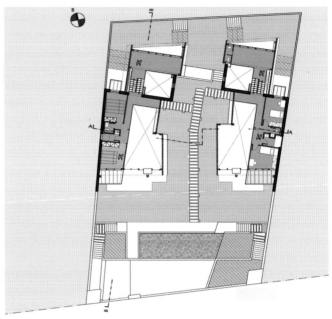

First floor plan

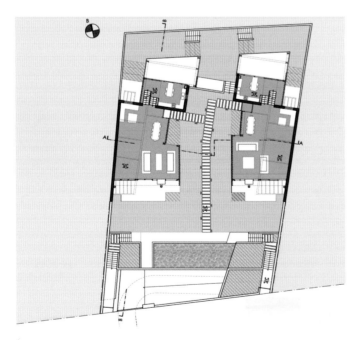

Ground floor plan

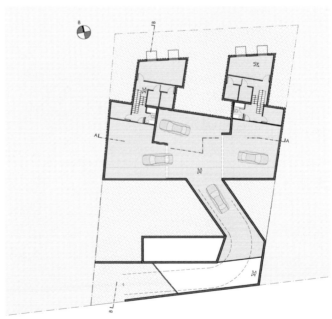

Basement plan

Site plan

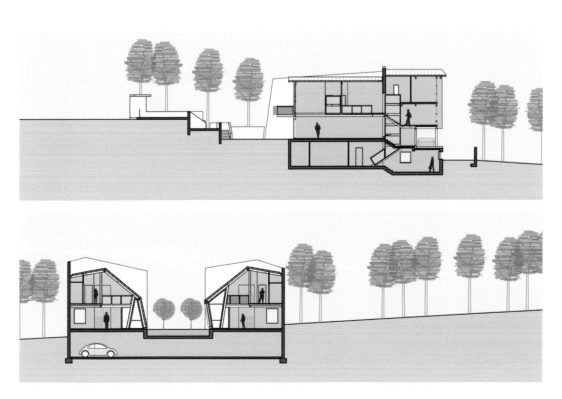

Sections

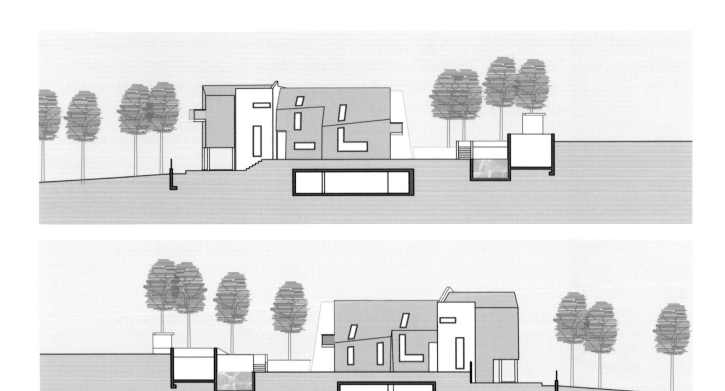

Elevations

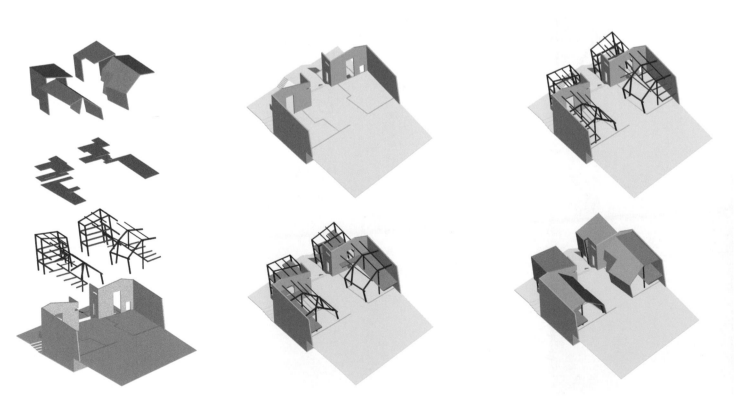

Axonometrics

BROKEN HOUSE

Katowice, Poland   2002

This strikingly designed house is located in Katowice, an important city in the historic region of Upper Silesia, Southern Poland, on the Klodnica and Rawa Rivers. It won the prize for best building in the city in 2003, and was chosen as one of the icons of Polish architecture in 2006.

The project is on a site near a forest, in mine-damaged land with tectonic faults. The site covers 37,700 sq ft (3,500 m²), on which a house was built with a floor area of 3,552 sq ft (330 m²). Such faults, with uplifted layers of soil interwoven with one another inspired the creativity of the project. The design is based on a series of solid rectangular volumes contrasted with a ribbon-like structure. The latter is a frame that emerges from the ground and winds around the volumes before returning to the ground. The ribbon is the predominant feature of the house. It connects a variety of spaces: from the pool to the living area, with a fireplace and the upstairs bedrooms. A major feature is the ramp, which eliminates the need for steps and forms an alternative vertical connection. This solution was achieved by altering the course, making it possible to keep the outer edges straight, without the bends that are typically found in these structures.

ARCHITECT
Robert Konieczny, Marlena Wolnik/
KWK PROMES

COLLABORATORS
Jaroslaw Kaminski
(structural engineering)

TOTAL SURFACE AREA
3,552 sq ft

PHOTOGRAPHY
© KWK PROMES

Known as Broken House, this residence features a ribbon-like structure. This feature connects a variety of spaces by means of a ramp that runs around the space, forming a vertical connection with the upper level of the building.

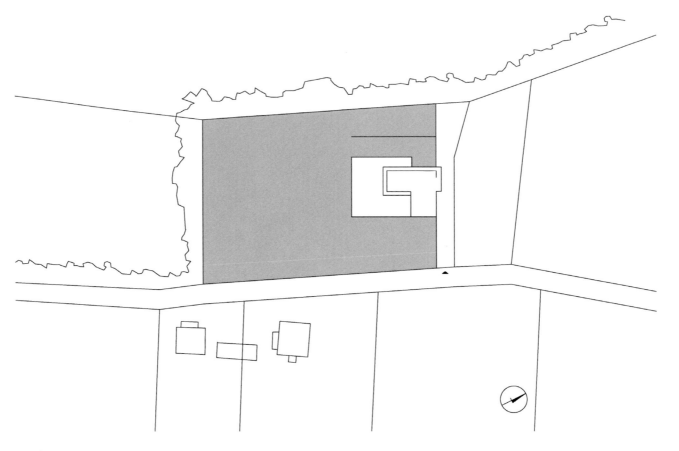

Site plan

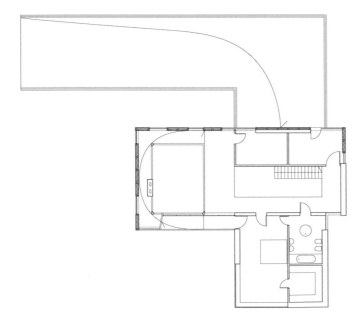

First floor plan

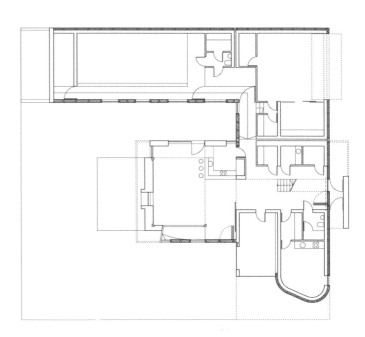

Ground floor plan

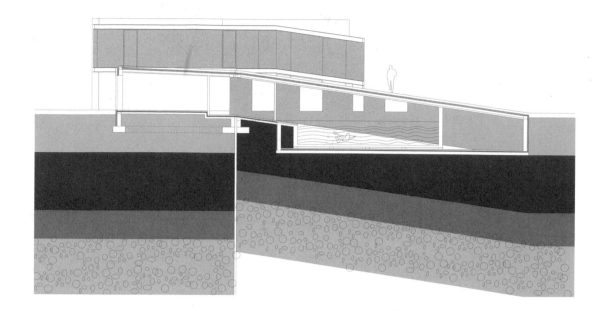

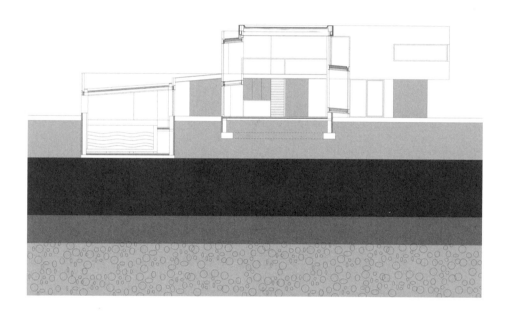

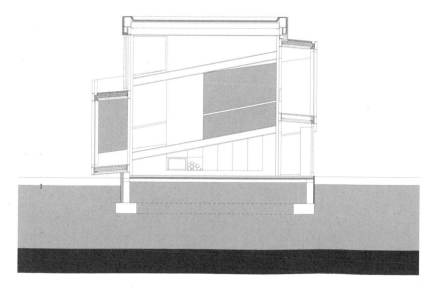

Sections

Directory

Andrés Remy Arquitectos
Buenos Aires, Argentina
www.andresremy.com

Andrés Silanes, Fernando Valderrama, Carlos Bañón/ SUBARQUITECTURA
Alicante, Spain
www.subarquitectura.com

Antje Osterwold, Matthias Schmidt/ Osterwold + Schmidt Architekten
Weimar, Germany
www.osterwold-schmidt.de

Antonino Cardillo Architect
Rome, Italy
www.antoninocardillo.com

Barton Myers Associates
Los Angeles, CA, USA
www.bartonmyers.com

BDA Architecture
Broadbeach, QLD, Australia
www.bdaarch.com.au

Belzberg Architects
Santa Monica, CA, USA
www.belzbergarchitects.com

BKK Architects
Melbourne, VIC, Australia
www.b-k-k.com.au

Brent Kendle/Kendle Design Collaborative
Scottsdale, AZ, USA
www.kendledesign.com

BUILD
Seattle, WA, USA
www.buildllc.com

Cass Smith, Sean Kennedy/ CCS Architecture
San Francisco, CA, USA
www.ccs-architecture.com

Christian Heiss, Michael Thomas, Thomas Mayer/Atelier Heiss
Vienna, Austria
www.atelier-heiss.at

Davide Macullo, Marco Strozzi/ Davide Macullo Architects
Lugano, Switzerland
www.macullo.com

Edward Szewczyk & Associates Architects
Woollahra, NSW, Australia
www.esa-architect.com.au

Eric Rosen Architects
Los Angeles, CA, USA
www.ericrosen.com

Ernst Havermans/ Oomen Architecten
Breda, The Netherlands
www.oomenarchitecten.nl

Fernando Forte, Lourenço Gimenes, Rodrigo Marcondes Ferraz/Forte, Gimenes & Marcondes Ferraz Arquitetos
São Paulo, Brazil
www.fgmf.com.br

Glen Irani Architects
Venice, CA, USA
www.glenirani.com

Griffin Enright Architects
Los Angeles, CA, USA
www.griffinenrightarchitects.com

Hyo Man Kim/IROJE KHM Architects
Seoul, South Korea
www.irojekhm.com

Javier Artadi/Artadi Arquitectos
Lima, Peru
www.javierartadi.com

Jesse Bornstein, Myungjong Lee/Bornarch
Santa Monica, CA, USA
www.bornarch.com

John Friedman Alice Kimm Architects
Los Angeles, CA, USA
www.jfak.net

Kevin deFreitas Architects
San Diego, CA, USA
www.defreitasarchitects.com

Marcio Kogan
São Paulo, Brazil
www.marciokogan.com.br

McIntosh Poris Associates
Birmingham, MI, USA
www.mcintoshporis.com

Min | Day
San Francisco, CA, USA
www.minday.com

Mole Architects
Ely, United Kingdom
www.molearchitects.co.uk

Montalba Architects
Santa Monica, CA, USA
www.montalbaarchitects.com

Nasser Abulhasan, Joaquín Pérez Goicoechea/AGi Architects
Madrid, Spain
www.agi-architects.com

Nikos Mesaritis, Marios Pelekanos/Polytia Armos
Nicosia, Cyprus
www.polytia.com

Nuno Mateus, José Mateus/ ARX Portugal Arquitectos
Lisbon, Portugal
www.arx.pt

Ogrydziak/Prillinger Architects
San Francisco, CA, USA
www.oparch.net

Paul McAneary, Mattias Laumayer/ Paul McAneary Architects
London, United Kingdom
www.paulmcaneary.com

Pitágoras Arquitectos
Guimarães, Portugal
www.pitagoras.pt

Pitman Tozer Architects
London, United Kingdom
www.pitmantozer.com

Powerhouse Company
Copenhagen, Denmark
www.powerhouse-company.com

React Architects
Anixi, Greece
www.re-act.gr

Robert Konieczny, Marlena Wolnik/KWK PROMES
Katowice, Poland
www.kwkpromes.pl

SHED Architecture & Design
Seattle, WA, USA
www.shedbuilt.com

Spiros Papadopoulos
Athens, Greece
www.spirospapadopoulos.net

Tony Owen Partners
Chippendale, NSW, Australia
www.tonyowen.com.au

UNStudio
Amsterdam, The Netherlands
www.unstudio.com

XTEN Architecture
Culver City, CA, USA
www.xtenarchitecture.com